Fifty Years of NFL Excitement

PHOTOGRAPHY

ABC-TV page 114; *John Betancourt* 175; *John Biever* 93; *Vernon Biever* 61, 86, 186, 187; *David Boss* 75, 99, 104, 155, 168; *Jim Chaffin* 177; *Thomas J. Croke* 173; Detroit News 8; *George Gellatly* 43, 187; *George Gojkovich* 123, 137, 141; *Pro Football Hall of Fame* 21, 22, 25, 26, 35, 62, 80; *Ken Hardin* 92; *Rod Hanna* 187; *Jocelyn Hinsen* 124; *Joe Kennedy* 150; *Bill Mark* 109; *Fred Matthes* 166; *John McDonough* 139; *Al Messerschmidt* 117; *Vic Milton* 165; *NFL Properties* 38, 129; *Dick Raphael* 97; *Russ Reed* 54, 71, 110, 153; *John Reid* 159; *Robert Riger* 56; *Frank Rippon* 44, 49, 59, 132; *Fred Roe* 95; *Ron Ross* 145; *Dan Rubin* 51; *Manny Rubio* 113; *Russ Russell* 182; *John Sandhaus* 161; *Carl Skalak, Jr.* 120; *Warren Skipper* 126; *Robert L. Smith* 119; *Jay Spencer* 186; *Bob Spinelli* 171; *Vic Stein* 29, 31, 40; *Dave Stock* 181; UPI 14, 18; *Bob Verlin* 89; *Herb Weitman* 83, 135, 178; *World Wide* 5.

ILLUSTRATIONS

Merv Corning pages 6, 11, 17, 33, 37, 47, 53, 67, 79, 101, 149.

First Printing, April 1986

Printed in the United States of America

INTRODUCTION

This book begins in 1934, the year Old Spice fragrance was introduced. It also was the year that the 15-year-old National Football League legalized forward passes from anywhere behind the line of scrimmage, paving the way for the wide-open style of football we know today.

Pro football had to battle to gain a spot in the American sports consciousness in 1934. Baseball and college football clearly were the dominant sports. There were 10 NFL franchises in 1934 (8 of them among the 28 that currently make up the league). The first league championship game had been played only two years before, the same year the detailed statistics and records that enhance our appreciation of the game officially had been recorded for the first time.

In the 1930s, NFL players were as tough as the leather of their helmets, rosters were small, and most were 60-minute men, playing both offense and defense. It was a time for legends, too, for men such as Bert Bell, Charles W. Bidwill, Sr., Joe Carr, Dutch Clark, Beattie Feathers, George Halas, Arnie Herber, Curly Lambeau, Tim Mara, George Preston Marshall, Bronko Nagurski, and Art Rooney.

You are correct if you noted that the title of this book is inaccurate. Since 1934, when the narrative begins, 52, not 50, NFL seasons have been played. Well, just as there have been more than 50 seasons, there has been more to the meteoric rise of pro football in that period than simply the excitement the title promises. Fact is, 1934 is only a point of departure, the opening kickoff to year after year of drama, personalities, and change. Even when the time on the field runs out, the game goes on and on.

1934

New beginnings—and one fond farewell—marked the 1934 NFL season.

Detroit radio station owner G.A. (Dick) Richards purchased the Portsmouth (Ohio) Spartans franchise and moved it to Detroit. Until that time, pro football had had a less-than-successful history in the Motor City; other teams had tried and folded there. But Richards, and his strong team, re-named the "Lions," were an immediate hit.

The annual Chicago All-Star Game was founded. The game, sponsored for charity by the *Chicago Tribune* and pitting the previous season's NFL champions against a team of college all-stars, got off to a rousing—and surprising—start before a crowd of 79,432 at Soldier Field on August 31. The Chicago Bears and the collegians played to a scoreless tie.

Chicago fullback Bronko Nagurski prepares to get the ball from Carl Brumbaugh in the "Sneakers Game" for the NFL title.

DEVELOPMENT OF THE UNIFORM

Mel Hein, Center, New York Giants *Numerals became necessary as the size of pro football squads increased. Soft, aviator-style ''glove'' helmets were disappearing in favor of reinforced leather hats that afforded more protection.*

The Bears then rolled to a 13-0 regular-season record with Bronko Nagurski and rookie tailback Beattie Feathers in the backfield. Feathers became the first pro back to rush for more than 1,000 yards in a season (1,004), and he missed three games, at that.

The Bears were heavily favored when they met the New York Giants on an icy field at the Polo Grounds for the NFL championship. They led 10-3 at halftime, but when the second half started, nine of the Giants were wearing sneakers. With better traction, the Giants ran away with the game, 30-13. The "Sneakers Game" became an instant NFL legend, and was considered a bigger upset than the one pulled earlier this same year by Max Baer when he knocked out Primo Carnera for the heavyweight championship.

In 1934, a full inch was taken off the girth of the football and the inflating pressure was reduced. The ball measured 21¼-21½ inches around and was inflated to a pressure of 12½-13½ pounds (the same as today's ball). Since 1925, the ball had slimmed down from an object with the approximate aerodynamic qualities of a melon to a streamlined missile. This, coupled with a new rule permitting forward passes anywhere behind the line of scrimmage, ushered in the modern passing game.

Future Hall of Famer Red Grange retired from pro football after a career as one of the early game's premier attractions.

The Cincinnati Reds franchise also had retired—in midseason. After losing eight straight games, the club disbanded and some of its former players moved to St. Louis, where they set up shop as the Gunners. The team played three games, losing two, and folded for good.

1934

EASTERN DIVISION

	W	L	T	Pct.	Pts.	OP
N.Y. Giants	8	5	0	.615	147	107
Boston	6	6	0	.500	107	94
Brooklyn	4	7	0	.364	61	153
Philadelphia	4	7	0	.364	127	85
Pittsburgh	2	10	0	.167	51	206

WESTERN DIVISION

	W	L	T	Pct.	Pts.	OP
Chi. Bears	13	0	0	1.000	286	86
Detroit	10	3	0	.769	238	59
Green Bay	7	6	0	.538	156	112
Chi. Cardinals	5	6	0	.455	80	84
St. Louis	1	2	0	.333	27	61
Cincinnati	0	8	0	.000	10	243

NFL championship: N.Y. GIANTS 30, Chi. Bears 13

1935

The NFL player limit in 1935 was 24 per team. Thus, one talented athlete could make a significant difference given such compact (by today's standards) rosters. This happened in Green Bay, when Don Hutson, a tall (6-1), slim (180 pounds), and fast (9.8 in the 100-yard dash) end from Alabama joined the Packers.

Detroit quarterback Earl (Dutch) Clark led the NFL in scoring.

On his first play as a pro, Hutson beat safety Beattie Feathers, caught a pass from quarterback Arnie Herber, and went 83 yards for a touchdown to help defeat the Bears 7-0. Herber and Hutson connected on 17 passes for seven touchdowns during the season, a preview of Hutson's coming glory. During his 11 seasons in the NFL, Hutson was the league's leading receiver eight times. His coach, Curly Lambeau, called him "the most valuable player to a team in the history of the game."

Despite Hutson, the Packers finished second in the NFL's Western Division in 1935 to the Detroit Lions. In only their second season in Detroit, the Lions secured their new territory—and their credibility—with a 26-7 victory over the New York Giants for the NFL title.

Pro football took another step toward a more wide-open, higher-scoring game by moving the inbounds lines, or hashmarks, nearer the center of the field, 15 yards in from the sidelines. This served to give offenses more room to operate in toward the near sideline, and gave field-goal kickers better angles.

The first night major league baseball game was played in 1935, 33 years after the first night football game. Other new institutions included the WPA, the China Clipper, and the roller derby.

1935

EASTERN DIVISION

	W	L	T	Pct.	Pts.	OP
N. Y. Giants	9	3	0	.750	180	96
Brooklyn	5	6	1	.455	90	141
Pittsburgh	4	8	0	.333	100	209
Boston	2	8	1	.200	65	123
Philadelphia	2	9	0	.182	60	179

WESTERN DIVISION

	W	L	T	Pct.	Pts.	OP
Detroit	7	3	2	.700	191	111
Green Bay	8	4	0	.667	181	96
Chi. Bears	6	4	2	.600	192	106
Chi. Cardinals	6	4	2	.600	99	97

NFL championship: DETROIT 26, N.Y. Giants 7
One game between Boston and Philadelphia was canceled.

1936

The first NFL college draft was held on February 8, 1936. The last-place team of 1935, the Philadelphia Eagles, drafted first, choosing University of Chicago back Jay Berwanger, the first Heisman Trophy winner. The Eagles later traded Berwanger's negotiating rights to Chicago, but Berwanger decided not to play pro football.

Things weren't all bad for Eagles co-owner Bert Bell, however. He acquired full ownership of the team, with its new 25-man roster limit, by paying his partner (and coach) Lud Wray $4,000.

Once the regular season started, Green Bay, with its Herber-to-Hutson passing combination, swept the league the same way Roosevelt swept Landon in the presidential election. The Packers defeated the Boston Redskins 21-6 in the NFL Championship Game, which was played in New York because Redskins owner George Preston Marshall was piqued at what he considered lack of support from his hometown fans.

The season saw no franchise shifts for the first time since the formation of the NFL, and for the first time all teams played the same number of games. All was not quiet in pro football, though. A rival six-team league was formed, the second to call itself the American Football League. Its inaugural champion was the Boston Shamrocks.

1936

EASTERN DIVISION

	W	L	T	Pct.	Pts.	OP
Boston	7	5	0	.583	149	110
Pittsburgh	6	6	0	.500	98	187
N.Y. Giants	5	6	1	.455	115	163
Brooklyn	3	8	1	.273	92	161
Philadelphia	1	11	0	.083	51	206

WESTERN DIVISION

	W	L	T	Pct.	Pts.	OP
Green Bay	10	1	1	.909	248	118
Chi. Bears	9	3	0	.750	222	94
Detroit	8	4	0	.667	235	102
Chi. Cardinals	3	8	1	.273	74	143

NFL championship: Green Bay 21, Boston 6, at Polo Grounds, N.Y.

DEVELOPMENT OF THE UNIFORM

Bronko Nagurski, Fullback, Chicago Bears *The league was stunned by the uniforms of the formerly conservative Bears. Never before had striping and color been so generously applied to jerseys, socks, and helmets. Much of it was gone the following season.*

1937

George Preston Marshall moved his team from Boston to Washington, D.C. There he became the sport's master showman, staging spectacular halftime shows and publicity gimmicks to stimulate interest in professional football. For example, when Marshall signed quarterback Sammy Baugh of TCU and introduced him to the Washington press corps, he outfitted him in a 10-gallon hat and cowboy boots, neither of which Baugh ever had worn before.

In his first season, "Slingin' Sammy" led the NFL in passing with 1,127 yards and 14 touchdowns, and teammate Cliff Battles was the top rusher with 874 yards as the Redskins swept through the Eastern Division, then upset the Bears for the league championship, 28-21. Thus began a great decade for the Redskins that included six divisional titles and another NFL championship.

Less heralded on the nation's sports pages was the return of pro football to Cleveland. Homer Marshman was granted a new franchise; general manager Buzz Wetzel named the team "Rams" (so that it would fit neatly in newspaper headlines). Unfortunately, the headlines were slow in coming for the team. The new Rams got off to an inauspicious start with a 1-10 record.

And speaking of inauspiciousness, the American Football League folded after two seasons of play. The 8-0 Los Angeles Bulldogs were its second, and last, championship team.

1937

EASTERN DIVISION	W	L	T	Pct.	Pts.	OP
Washington	8	3	0	.727	195	120
N.Y. Giants	6	3	2	.667	128	109
Pittsburgh	4	7	0	.364	122	145
Brooklyn	3	7	1	.300	82	174
Philadelphia	2	8	1	.200	86	177

WESTERN DIVISION	W	L	T	Pct.	Pts.	OP
Chi. Bears	9	1	1	.900	201	100
Green Bay	7	4	0	.636	220	122
Detroit	7	4	0	.636	180	105
Chi. Cardinals	5	5	1	.500	135	165
Cleveland	1	10	0	.091	75	207

NFL championship: Washington 28, CHI. BEARS 21

1938

The panic felt in Green Bay when it was learned that Don Hutson was injured prior to the NFL title game against the Eastern Division-champion New York Giants was second only to that felt in New Jersey this year when Orson Welles broadcast his famous hoax of an invasion from Mars, "War of the Worlds."

Green Bay's panic turned out to be rooted in reality. Hutson was able to limp on to the Polo Grounds for only a few plays, and the Giants pleased most of the 48,120 fans by winning the NFL championship 23-17.

Byron (Whizzer) White of the Pittsburgh Steelers, who later became a Supreme Court Justice, was the NFL's leading rusher with 567 yards.

Hugh L. (Shorty) Ray began his work that aided football's evolution into the modern era. Long interested in streamlining and organizing football rules, Ray was hired by the NFL in a part-time advisory capacity. His function was to consult with officials and to make studies of the game with an eye toward improving the rules, which were changing in response to the increased importance of the passing game. One newly-adopted ruled included a fifteen-yard penalty for roughing the passer.

Perhaps prompted by the success of the Chicago All-Star Game, Los Angeles newspaper officials announced the establishment of the Pro Bowl, a game to be played between the new NFL champion and a team made up of league all-stars.

1938

EASTERN DIVISION

	W	L	T	Pct.	Pts.	OP
N.Y. Giants	8	2	1	.800	194	79
Washington	6	3	2	.667	148	154
Brooklyn	4	4	3	.500	131	161
Philadelphia	5	6	0	.455	154	164
Pittsburgh	2	9	0	.182	79	169

WESTERN DIVISION

	W	L	T	Pct.	Pts.	OP
Green Bay	8	3	0	.727	223	118
Detroit	7	4	0	.636	119	108
Chi. Bears	6	5	0	.545	194	148
Cleveland	4	7	0	.364	131	215
Chi. Cardinals	2	9	0	.182	111	168

NFL championship: N.Y. GIANTS 23, Green Bay 17

1939

The New York Giants, fresh from their championship victory over the Green Bay Packers, defeated the Pro All-Stars in the first Pro Bowl game, at Wrigley Field in Los Angeles on January 15.

Joe F. Carr, NFL president for 19 years, died in Columbus, Ohio, where he had established league head-

Cecil Isbell (17) rifles a pass to end Don Hutson for a 10-yard gain against the Giants in the 1939 NFL Championship Game.

quarters upon his selection in 1921. His drive and optimism were significant as he nurtured the sport to stability and success. Carl L. Storck, league secretary during Carr's tenure, succeeded Carr as president.

Pro football entered the television age on October 22, 1939. That Sunday afternoon, NBC television station W2XBS broadcast a game between the Philadelphia Eagles and the Brooklyn Dodgers from Brooklyn's Ebbets Field, the first professional football game ever televised. At the time, there were approximately 1,000 television sets in the New York viewing area to receive announcer Bill Walz's play-by-play, until the daylight—and with it the picture—dimmed.

World War II, in its first months, seemed far removed from Milwaukee, where coach Curly Lambeau moved the NFL Championship Game between his Packers and the New York Giants. The Giants were bombed, 27-0, by a team which was considered Lambeau's strongest. Fans were charged $4.40 per ticket, a new high for pro football, but that didn't seem to hurt attendance. The game sold out in two days.

1939

EASTERN DIVISION	W	L	T	Pct.	Pts.	OP
N.Y. Giants	9	1	1	.900	168	85
Washington	8	2	1	.800	242	94
Brooklyn	4	6	1	.400	108	219
Philadelphia	1	9	1	.100	105	200
Pittsburgh	1	9	1	.100	114	216

WESTERN DIVISION	W	L	T	Pct.	Pts.	OP
Green Bay	9	2	0	.818	233	153
Chi. Bears	8	3	0	.727	298	157
Detroit	6	5	0	.545	145	150
Cleveland	5	5	1	.500	195	164
Chi. Cardinals	1	10	0	.091	84	254

NFL championship: GREEN BAY 27, N.Y. Giants 0

Never mind Cleveland Indians pitcher Bob Feller's opening day no-hitter against the Chicago White Sox. Forget Cornelius Warmerdam being the first man to pole vault 15 feet. Don't even mention Wilbur Shaw winning his third Indianapolis 500. The sports story of this year was the 73-0 shellacking given the Washington Redskins by the Chicago Bears in the NFL Championship Game.

The score still stands as the largest margin of victory in NFL history. Chicago, playing the T-formation with a man in motion, used quick openers counter to the flow of play. With quarterback Sid Luckman directing the attack, 10 Bears players scored touchdowns. To make the final score all the more incredible, the Redskins had beaten Chicago 7-3 three weeks earlier and were favored in the game.

This game, and Stanford's Rose Bowl victory over Nebraska three weeks later, helped convince college and high school teams all across the country to utilize the quick-opening T-formation. The formation was developed and refined by Bears coach George Halas, former Bears coach Ralph Jones, and Clark Shaughnessy, the Stanford coach who had formed a close association with Halas while coaching at the University of Chicago.

The game also was noteworthy because it was the first NFL championship carried on network radio, broadcast by Red Barber to 120 stations of the Mutual Broadcasting System, which paid $2,500 for the rights.

Fred L. Mandel, Jr., purchased the Detroit franchise from Dick Richards, and Alexis Thompson purchased the Pittsburgh franchise (changing its name from Pirates to Steelers) from Art Rooney, who later bought a half interest in the Philadelphia Eagles.

The Eagles had a diminutive (150 pounds) rookie passer, Davey O'Brien. He conducted a one-man, one-game crusade for the forward pass, throwing 60 times in a game against Washington, completing 33.

DEVELOPMENT OF THE UNIFORM

Byron (Whizzer) White, Halfback, Detroit Lions
Light and strong new fabrics were being incorporated into football uniforms (nylon, rayon, and cotton were the most popular) in identifiable team colors, such as the Lions' Honolulu blue and silver.

Head coach George Halas and his Bears celebrate their 73-0 victory over the Redskins for the NFL championship.

The third incarnation of an American Football League formed. It had six teams. Like its predecessor, it folded after two seasons of play.

1940

EASTERN DIVISION	W	L	T	Pct.	Pts.	OP
Washington	9	2	0	.818	245	142
Brooklyn	8	3	0	.727	186	120
N.Y. Giants	6	4	1	.600	131	133
Pittsburgh	2	7	2	.222	60	178
Philadelphia	1	10	0	.091	111	211

WESTERN DIVISION	W	L	T	Pct.	Pts.	OP
Chi. Bears	8	3	0	.727	238	152
Green Bay	6	4	1	.600	238	155
Detroit	5	5	1	.500	138	153
Cleveland	4	6	1	.400	171	191
Chi. Cardinals	2	7	2	.222	139	222

NFL championship: Chi. Bears 73, WASHINGTON 0

The magic of the Bears' 1940 championship T-party over the Redskins carried over to the next season as 98,203 stormed Soldier Field to see Chicago roll over the College All-Stars 37-13 in the annual August game.

Elmer Layden, head coach and athletic director at Notre Dame and one of the legendary "Four Horsemen," had become the first NFL Commissioner in March. He moved league headquarters to Chicago. President/secretary Carl Storck resigned a month later.

Co-owners Bert Bell and Art Rooney exchanged their Philadelphia franchise for Alexis Thompson's in Pittsburgh. Homer Marshman sold his Cleveland Rams to Daniel F. Reeves and Fred Levy, Jr., on June 1.

It took Japan's sneak attack on Pearl Harbor to arrest pro football's meteoric rise to the top of the sports world. On that fateful December 7, there were 43,425 at Wrigley Field to see the Bears beat the Green Bay Packers 33-14 in the first divisional playoff game in NFL history. News of the Japanese attack reached the press box at halftime.

On December 21, the Bears, who had beaten the Packers 33-14 a week earlier in the first divisional playoff game in NFL history, played the Giants for the NFL championship. With the war two weeks old, only 13,341 showed up to see Chicago take its fifth title, 39-7. Nevertheless, league attendance passed the million mark for the third consecutive year.

1941

EASTERN DIVISION

	W	L	T	Pct.	Pts.	OP
N.Y. Giants	8	3	0	.727	238	114
Brooklyn	7	4	0	.636	158	127
Washington	6	5	0	.545	176	174
Philadelphia	2	8	1	.200	119	218
Pittsburgh	1	9	1	.100	103	276

WESTERN DIVISION

	W	L	T	Pct.	Pts.	OP
Chi. Bears	10	1	0	.909	396	147
Green Bay	10	1	0	.909	258	120
Detroit	4	6	1	.400	121	195
Chi. Cardinals	3	7	1	.300	127	197
Cleveland	2	9	0	.182	116	244

Western Division playoff: CHI. BEARS 33, Green Bay 14
NFL championship: CHI. BEARS 37, N.Y. Giants 9

Players departing for service in World War II severely reduced the rosters of NFL teams. In the Western Division, Chicago coach George Halas was called for Navy duty prior to the NFL title game, joining many of his players. Hunk Anderson and Luke Johnsos began a four-year stint as co-coaches after the remnants of that great Bears team had compiled a regular-season record of 11-0.

In the Eastern Division, the Redskins lost only once and came into the championship game with just one thought: to avenge the 73-0 humiliation suffered two seasons before. They did it, 14-6, as Sammy Baugh passed to Wilbur Moore for one touchdown and Andy Farkas ran for another.

In Green Bay, Don Hutson was still on a rampage. He caught a record 74 passes, 17 of them for touchdowns. Packers quarterback Cecil Isbell became the first man in NFL history to pass for more than 2,000 yards.

1942

EASTERN DIVISION

	W	L	T	Pct.	Pts.	OP
Washington	10	1	0	.909	227	102
Pittsburgh	7	4	0	.636	167	119
N.Y. Giants	5	5	1	.500	155	139
Brooklyn	3	8	0	.273	100	168
Philadelphia	2	9	0	.182	134	239

WESTERN DIVISION

	W	L	T	Pct.	Pts.	OP
Chi. Bears	11	0	0	1.000	376	84
Green Bay	8	2	1	.800	300	215
Cleveland	5	6	0	.455	150	207
Chi. Cardinals	3	8	0	.273	98	209
Detroit	0	11	0	.000	38	263

NFL championship: WASHINGTON 14, Chi. Bears 6

Green Bay's Don Hutson stretches for a catch against Detroit.

1943

The lack of manpower was sorely felt all around the league. Lieutenant Dan Reeves and Major Fred Levy, being in no position to run a team, asked (and received) permission to temporarily halt operations of the Cleveland Rams. Ten days later, Levy transferred his stock in the team to Reeves.

"Slingin'" Sammy Baugh of the Washington Redskins.

Philadelphia and Pittsburgh, in similar straits, combined forces and played as the Phil-Pitt "Steagles". The merged team, under co-coaches Greasy Neale and Walt Kiesling, divided home games between the two cities. The merger automatically dissolved on the last day of the season.

Players not in military service were distributed around the league, and free substitution was voted in for the duration of the war.

In the West, Bronko Nagurski came out of a six-year retirement to lead his old team, the Chicago Bears, to the divisional title. Sid Luckman still had a hot hand. He passed for seven touchdowns in one regular-season game against the New York Giants.

In the East, the champion Redskins beat the Giants, 28-0, in a divisional playoff game. But they lost their NFL title to the 35-year-old Nagurski, playing his last game, and the Bears, 41-21.

Despite the impact of the war, some still saw room in pro football for expansion. Ted Collins was granted a franchise for Boston beginning in 1944.

1943

EASTERN DIVISION	W	L	T	Pct.	Pts.	OP	WESTERN DIVISION	W	L	T	Pct.	Pts.	OP
Washington	6	3	1	.667	229	137	Chi. Bears	8	1	1	.889	303	157
N.Y. Giants	6	3	1	.667	197	170	Green Bay	7	2	1	.778	264	172
Phil-Pitt	5	4	1	.556	225	230	Detroit	3	6	1	.333	178	218
Brooklyn	2	8	0	.200	65	234	Chi. Cardinals	0	10	0	.000	95	238

Eastern Division playoff: Washington 28, N.Y. GIANTS 0
NFL championship: CHI. BEARS 41, Washington 21

1944

The war continued to utilize most of the able-bodied, but there were enough players available to keep the NFL in business. Many of the players were in the service, but were allowed passes on weekends just for the games. Others were working in essential industries, but were able to play on Sundays and attend limited practices in off-hours.

The manpower shortage was so great that only 12 of the 330 players selected in the NFL draft actually played for their teams in 1944. Many teams brought players out of retirement; center Mel Hein, kicker Ken Strong, and former Packers tailback Arnie Herber were re-activated by the Giants.

The shuffling of teams continued. The new Boston franchise was named the Yanks, because owner Ted Collins had wanted a team for Yankee Stadium in New York. The Brooklyn Dodgers changed their name to Tigers. Cleveland resumed full operations.

The Philadelphia-Pittsburgh merger was dissolved and the Eagles began to operate on their own once more. But Pittsburgh still was shorthanded. It merged again, this time with the Chicago Cardinals, and played under the name Card-Pitt for the season.

Coach Curly Lambeau won his sixth—and final—championship with Green Bay. The Packers defeated the Giants 14-7 in the title game.

1944

EASTERN DIVISION

	W	L	T	Pct.	Pts.	OP
N.Y. Giants	8	1	1	.889	206	75
Philadelphia	7	1	2	.875	267	131
Washington	6	3	1	.667	169	180
Boston	2	8	0	.200	82	233
Brooklyn	0	10	0	.000	69	166

WESTERN DIVISION

	W	L	T	Pct.	Pts.	OP
Green Bay	8	2	0	.800	238	141
Chi. Bears	6	3	1	.667	258	172
Detroit	6	3	1	.667	216	151
Cleveland	4	6	0	.400	188	224
Card-Pitt	0	10	0	.000	108	328

NFL championship: Green Bay 14, N.Y. GIANTS 7

Soldiers wounded in action in World War II watch a New York Giants game from a special section on the sideline. Many of the players they were watching had to get special passes from their military units to join their teams on Sundays for games.

1945

The NFL celebrated the end of the war, but there was cause for mourning, too. Of men who had played in NFL games, 638 served in World War II, 355 as commissioned officers. Sixty-six were decorated, and 21 lost their lives.

As in the rest of the country, things began getting back to normal. George Halas returned from naval duty in the Pacific and resumed coaching the Bears. Hashmarks were moved five yards nearer the center of the

The Redskins were on the wrong end of the thermometer as well as the score in the 1945 NFL Championship Game in Cleveland.

field, now 20 yards from the sidelines. And, true to form, there were more franchise shifts. The Boston Yanks and Brooklyn Tigers merged in Boston as the Yanks.

Quarterback Bob Waterfield of UCLA joined the Cleveland Rams and confused opponents with his adeptness on the bootleg play. The rookie's finesse helped the Rams to the Western Division title, while in the East, Washington beat out Philadelphia.

The Rams and Redskins met in Cleveland for the NFL championship on a day so cold that the instruments of the famed Redskins band froze. Waterfield led the Rams, who never had had a season over the .500 mark before, to the title with a 15-14 win. Washington quarterback Sammy Baugh, however, provided the Rams with their margin of victory. Trying to pass out of his own end zone, he hit the goal post with the ball—an automatic safety. The rule was changed the next season.

Attendance climbed back over the million mark. Pressure mounted to expand the league, but the old guard was wary. More than 40 franchises had folded since the original formation of the NFL in 1920, twelve of them in one season after an earlier, premature attempt at expansion. The three American Football League fiascos loomed large. The NFL stood pat.

1945

EASTERN DIVISION

	W	L	T	Pct.	Pts.	OP
Washington	8	2	0	.800	209	121
Philadelphia	7	3	0	.700	272	133
N.Y. Giants	3	6	1	.333	179	198
Boston	3	6	1	.333	123	211
Pittsburgh	2	8	0	.200	79	220

WESTERN DIVISION

	W	L	T	Pct.	Pts.	OP
Cleveland	9	1	0	.900	244	136
Detroit	7	3	0	.700	195	194
Green Bay	6	4	0	.600	258	173
Chi. Bears	3	7	0	.300	192	235
Chi. Cardinals	1	9	0	.100	98	228

NFL championship: CLEVELAND 15, Washington 14

1946

The NFL became a coast-to-coast league for the first time. Dan Reeves, recognizing the vast potential in southern California, petitioned the league to allow his champion Cleveland Rams to move to Los Angeles. He was turned down by the other owners at first, but they relented when Reeves pointed out that he lost $50,000 with a championship club in Cleveland and would sell his franchise if forced to stay in Ohio. Reeves's sagacity was revealed when, in their first game in Los Angeles, a rematch with the Washington Redskins, the Rams attracted a crowd of 95,000.

Elmer Layden resigned as commissioner and Bert Bell, one of the Pittsburgh owners, was given the job and a three-year contract. Bell, who had handled every phase of the club operation both in Philadelphia and Pittsburgh, from hawking tickets to coaching the team, knew about club problems and had the personality to obtain the necessary cooperation from a dozen independent owners. League headquarters were moved to the Philadelphia suburb of Bala Cynwyd.

But problems cropped up for Bell from outside the NFL. A new rival league formed, the All-America Football Conference, with teams in Buffalo, Brooklyn, Los Angeles, Miami, Chicago, New York, San Francisco, and Cleveland. Four AAFC clubs shared markets with NFL teams, and a wage war was precipitated between the leagues for players. Few graduating college players could afford to pass up playing pro football.

Both leagues did fairly well in overall attendance—about 1.7 million each—but certain franchises ran into trouble. In the AAFC, Miami went under and was replaced by Baltimore.

In the NFL, the New York Giants had to battle two of the new league's teams for spectators, playing dates, and players. The Giants had more trouble when backs Frank Filchock and Merle Hapes were questioned about an attempt by a New York man to fix the upcoming cham-

Kenny Washington (13) broke the color line in Los Angeles.

pionship game between the Giants and Chicago. Commissioner Bell suspended Filchock for not immediately reporting the incident. Hapes was allowed to play in the game (won by the Bears 24-14), but was suspended thereafter.

Pro football broke the color line when UCLA's Kenny Washington became the first black player to sign with a major league athletic team since the 1920s. Washington and Woody Strode played for the Rams. Marion Motley and Bill Willis played for the Browns, who were the AAFC'c first champions.

1946

EASTERN DIVISION	W	L	T	Pct.	Pts.	OP	WESTERN DIVISION	W	L	T	Pct.	Pts.	OP
N.Y. Giants	7	3	1	.700	236	162	Chi. Bears	8	2	1	.800	289	193
Philadelphia	6	5	0	.545	231	220	Los Angeles	6	4	1	.600	277	257
Washington	5	5	1	.500	171	191	Green Bay	6	5	0	.545	148	158
Pittsburgh	5	5	1	.500	136	117	Chi. Cardinals	6	5	0	.545	260	198
Boston	2	8	1	.200	189	273	Detroit	1	10	0	.091	142	310

NFL championship: Chi. Bears 24, N.Y. GIANTS 14

1947

The Chicago Cardinals, the oldest club in pro football in point of continuous operation, won their first NFL championship since 1925 with their "Million Dollar Backfield" of Paul Christman (Missouri), Pat Harder (Wisconsin), Charley Trippi (Georgia), and Elmer Angsman (Notre Dame). Christman passed for more than 2,000 yards and 17 touchdowns during the season, then led the Cardinals past Steve Van Buren and the Philadelphia Eagles, 28-21, in the NFL Championship Game.

In the AAFC, mastermind Paul Brown guided the Cleveland Browns to their second straight championship behind the passing of quarterback Otto Graham and the running of fullback Marion Motley.

Both leagues drew well—about 1.8 million each—but it was not enough. Only Cleveland made money in the AAFC, and many NFL teams were struggling to show a profit.

NFL rules added a fifth official, the back judge, on the field. And, to eliminate the possibility of postseason ties, sudden death overtime was re-adopted for championship games; the first team to score in the extra period would win.

1947

EASTERN DIVISION

	W	L	T	Pct.	Pts.	OP
Philadelphia	8	4	0	.667	308	242
Pittsburgh	8	4	0	.667	240	259
Boston	4	7	1	.364	168	256
Washington	4	8	0	.333	295	367
N.Y. Giants	2	8	2	.200	190	309

WESTERN DIVISION

	W	L	T	Pct.	Pts.	OP
Chi. Cardinals	9	3	0	.750	306	231
Chi. Bears	8	4	0	.667	363	241
Green Bay	6	5	1	.545	274	210
Los Angeles	6	6	0	.500	259	214
Detroit	3	9	0	.250	231	305

Eastern Division playoff: Philadelphia 21, PITTSBURGH 0
NFL championship: CHI. CARDINALS 28, Philadelphia 21

Charley Trippi of the Cardinals' "Million Dollar Backfield."

1948

In a year of upsets, Truman beat Dewey, Marcel Cerdan took Tony Zale's middleweight boxing title, and a California schoolboy, Bob Mathias, won the Olympic decathlon gold medal in London.

In pro football, though, predictability reigned. The NFL-champion Chicago Cardinals ripped through the Western Division with an 11-1 record. In the East, the Philadelphia Eagles also repeated, setting up a rematch of the 1947 title game. It was played in Philadelphia's Shibe Park in a blinding snow storm. Incredibly, 36,309 showed up to watch the Eagles prevail, 7-0, after recovering a fumble on the Cardinals' 17-yard line. Steve Van Buren scored the touchdown.

In the AAFC, Cleveland continued its dominance by winning 15 straight games and its third consecutive championship. A notable addition to the Baltimore franchise was quarterback Y.A. Tittle, who completed 55 percent of his passes for 2,522 yards and 16 touchdowns. But a drop in attendance that affected both leagues resulted in a Brooklyn-New York AAFC merger for the 1949 season.

The NFL's Detroit Lions were sold again, this time to a syndicate headed by D. Lyle Fife.

1948

EASTERN DIVISION	W	L	T	Pct.	Pts.	OP
Philadelphia	9	2	1	.818	376	156
Washington	7	5	0	.583	291	287
N.Y. Giants	4	8	0	.333	297	388
Pittsburgh	4	8	0	.333	200	243
Boston	3	9	0	.250	174	372

WESTERN DIVISION	W	L	T	Pct.	Pts.	OP
Chi. Cardinals	11	1	0	.917	395	226
Chi. Bears	10	2	0	.833	375	151
Los Angeles	6	5	1	.545	327	269
Green Bay	3	9	0	.250	154	290
Detroit	2	10	0	.167	200	407

NFL championship: PHILADELPHIA 7, Chi. Cardinals 0

DEVELOPMENT OF THE UNIFORM

Bob Waterfield, Quarterback, Los Angeles Rams
When halfback Fred Gehrke painted Rams horns on his leather helmet in 1948, he created an immediate sensation—and a rash of imitators. Today, only the Cleveland Browns have helmets without team logos.

1949

The impact of NFL rulesmaker Hugh (Shorty) Ray was becoming evident. Among Ray's more unexpected discoveries, from his detailed chart and stopwatch observations, was that the faster a football game was played, the longer it took. In other words, the quicker that plays were run off, the more chances there were to stop the clock, and the longer the game lasted.

Ray worked hard with officials to expedite their handling of the game. Consequently, the NFL now ran off many more plays per game. Ray instigated so many rules changes that pro and college football had major differences in 150 rules after being nearly identical a decade before. Most of the changes opened up the action so that the pros averaged more than five touchdowns per game, up from 2.7 in 1936. Ray's final major battle was for free substitution; the NFL voted to try it on a one-year basis, thus moving pro football into the era of specialization and 60-minute action.

On the playing field, Steve Van Buren, Bosh Pritchard, Tommy Thompson, and the rest of the awesome Philadelphia Eagles rolled through the Eastern Division. Then, in a driving rain, the mudder Eagles overpowered the thoroughbred Rams 14-0 for the NFL championship.

Los Angeles coach Clark Shaughnessy had introduced the flanker or "third end" to football. Already blessed with two good receivers in Tom Fears and Bob Shaw, Shaughnessy split halfback Elroy (Crazylegs) Hirsch (newly acquired from the AAFC's Chicago Rockets) out wide. Years later, every team in pro football used the formation.

Cleveland won yet another AAFC title, beating San Francisco 21-7 in the championship game.

Though Congress had passed a law raising the minimum wage from 40 to 75 cents an hour, it evidently was not enough to boost attendance at Sunday football games. Each league suffered another drop at the gate. Following the season, Commissioner Bert Bell and

Steve Van Buren was a battering ram for the powerful Eagles.

AAFC representative J. Arthur Friedlund announced a merger of the two leagues. The new league retained the name National Football League, and Bell remained its commissioner. Three AAFC teams were absorbed intact by the NFL—the Cleveland Browns, San Francisco 49ers, and Baltimore Colts. The other four clubs were disbanded and their players dealt to the surviving teams.

1949

EASTERN DIVISION

	W	L	T	Pct.	Pts.	OP
Philadelphia	11	1	0	.917	364	134
Pittsburgh	6	5	1	.545	224	214
N.Y. Giants	6	6	0	.500	287	298
Washington	4	7	1	.364	268	339
N.Y. Bulldogs	1	10	1	.091	153	365

WESTERN DIVISION

	W	L	T	Pct.	Pts.	OP
Los Angeles	8	2	2	.800	360	239
Chi. Bears	9	3	0	.750	332	218
Chi. Cardinals	6	5	1	.545	360	301
Detroit	4	8	0	.333	237	259
Green Bay	2	10	0	.167	114	329

NFL championship: Philadelphia 14, LOS ANGELES 0

On the football scene, the war between the NFL and AAFC was over. On the world scene, the Korean War began.

The expanded National Football League was realigned into the American Conference (predominantly eastern), including the Chicago Cardinals, Cleveland Browns, New York Giants, Philadelphia Eagles, Pittsburgh Steelers, and Washington Redskins; and the National Conference (predominantly western), including the Baltimore Colts, Chicago Bears, Detroit Lions, Green Bay Packers, Los Angeles Rams, New York Yanks, and San Francisco 49ers.

Cleveland, needing no time for adjustment to NFL play, went on to tie New York for the conference title, then defeated the Giants 8-3 in a playoff to win the American Conference. Out on the west coast, the Rams beat the Bears 28-14 in a playoff to win the National Conference and a trip to Cleveland. The championship game was played in freezing weather before 29,751 hardy spectators who watched the two teams trade touchdowns all afternoon. With 28 seconds left, Lou Groza kicked a 16-yard field goal and the Browns won the NFL championship 30-28 in their first year in the league.

Like the Browns, All-America halfback Doak Walker of SMU had something to prove to the NFL. He joined the Detroit Lions as a rookie, led the league in scoring with 128 points, and silenced critics who said he was too small to play pro football.

Dan Reeves, owner of the Rams, proved something, too. He allowed every Los Angeles game, home and away, to be televised. Los Angeles fans responded by staying in their living rooms every Sunday. Rams records showed 105,109 total attendance in 1950—100,000 less than the previous season. Reeves ended his experiment with television, putting a home blackout in effect in 1951. The local television contract and blackout concepts spread rapidly in pro football, strengthening the electronic bond between the sport and the medium.

DEVELOPMENT OF THE UNIFORM

Marion Motley, Fullback, Cleveland Browns *Until 1952, when a ruling affected numbering, a player could wear any number he pleased. Today, each position has its own range of numbers. For example, Motley would have to wear a number between 20 and 49.*

Quarterback Otto Graham helped the Browns, newly absorbed from the defunct AAFC, win their first NFL championship.

1950

AMERICAN CONFERENCE

	W	L	T	Pct.	Pts.	OP
Cleveland	10	2	0	.833	310	144
N.Y. Giants	10	2	0	.833	268	150
Philadelphia	6	6	0	.500	254	141
Pittsburgh	6	6	0	.500	180	195
Chi. Cardinals	5	7	0	.417	233	287
Washington	3	9	0	.250	232	326

NATIONAL CONFERENCE

	W	L	T	Pct.	Pts.	OP
Los Angeles	9	3	0	.750	466	309
Chi. Bears	9	3	0	.750	279	207
N.Y. Yanks	7	5	0	.583	366	367
Detroit	6	6	0	.500	321	285
Green Bay	3	9	0	.250	244	406
San Francisco	3	9	0	.250	213	300
Baltimore	1	11	0	.083	213	462

American Conference playoff: CLEVELAND 8, N.Y. Giants 3
National Conference playoff: LOS ANGELES 24, Chi. Bears 14
NFL championship: CLEVELAND 30, Los Angeles 28

The Pro Bowl game, dormant since 1942, was revived in January at the Los Angeles Coliseum with a new format matching all-star teams from each conference. In the first game of the new series, the American Conference defeated the National Conference 28-27.

Later that month, Abraham Watner returned his Baltimore Colts franchise and player contracts to the league for $50,000. The Colts players, Y.A. Tittle among them, were included in the regular college draft.

The talent-rich Los Angeles Rams had come back hungry from their championship game loss to Cleveland, and were anxious for the new season to begin. With Bob Waterfield and Norm Van Brocklin sharing the quarterbacking, Tom Fears and Elroy Hirsch doing the receiving, and a potent corps of running backs that included Dan Towler, Tank Younger, Dick Hoerner, Verda (Vitamin T.) Smith, and Glenn Davis, the Rams stormed through their schedule. They gained 5,506 yards during the regular season, including 735 in one explosion against the New York Yanks. Hirsch led the league with 66 receptions (17 for touchdowns), and Waterfield was the NFL's top passer.

Meanwhile, Cleveland was dominating the American Conference with an 11-1 record. After winning five consecutive championships in five years of existence, the Browns were well prepared to defend their latest title when they headed west for a much-anticipated championship rematch in Los Angeles. The record crowd of 57,522, plus the first coast-to-coast championship game television audience, was not disappointed. The Rams won the hard-fought game, 24-17, on a fourth-quarter, perfect 73-yard pass from Van Brocklin to Fears.

Thanks to teams such as Los Angeles, the passing game had prospered. But the league saw fit to keep it from getting out of hand; the rules committee made centers, tackles, and guards ineligible pass receivers, even when on the end of the line.

Rams end Elroy (Crazylegs) Hirsch topped league receivers.

1951

AMERICAN CONFERENCE	W	L	T	Pct.	Pts.	OP
Cleveland	11	1	0	.917	331	152
N.Y. Giants	9	2	1	.818	254	161
Washington	5	7	0	.417	183	296
Pittsburgh	4	7	1	.364	183	235
Philadelphia	4	8	0	.333	234	264
Chi. Cardinals	3	9	0	.250	210	287

NATIONAL CONFERENCE	W	L	T	Pct.	Pts.	OP
Los Angeles	8	4	0	.667	392	261
Detroit	7	4	1	.636	336	259
San Francisco	7	4	1	.636	255	205
Chi. Bears	7	5	0	.583	286	282
Green Bay	3	9	0	.250	254	375
N.Y. Yanks	1	9	2	.100	241	382

NFL championship: LOS ANGELES 24, Cleveland 17

1952

The New York Yanks' checkered past caught up with them on January 19. After eight seasons spent variously as the Boston Yanks and New York Bulldogs and Yanks, the franchise was sold back to the league by Ted Collins. A new franchise was created to replace it, one that became the first NFL team in Texas, the Dallas Texans. Despite a transfusion given by the Rams, who traded 11 men to the Texans for Army Lieutenant Les Richter (who wasn't even available for two more years), the franchise didn't fare any better than its defunct predecessor. It was turned back to the league during the season and finished out its schedule on the road. The team did not disappear without gaining a modicum of distinction: It was thc last NFL team to become extinct.

Speaking of extinction, the Pittsburgh Steelers abandoned the Single Wing for the T-Formation, the last pro team to do so.

(In the early years of the NFL, most teams used the Single Wing formation, which had been pioneered by Glenn S. [Pop] Warner and brought into pro football by Jim Thorpe of the Canton Bulldogs in 1916. The Single Wing had four backs, the most important of which was the left halfback, or tailback. Early tailbacks, such as Sammy Baugh [who became a quarterback when the Redskins switched to the T-Formation in 1945] and Dutch Clark called the signals, received most of the snaps from center, ran, passed, and, frequently, kicked. The right halfback, or wingback, in the Single Wing lined up outside the right end and primarily was a blocker, but also ran with the ball, most notably on the inside reverse. The fullback was a burly up-the-middle runner who also received the snap occasionally. Unlike today's quarterback, the Single Wing quarterback was simply a blocking back who considered one carry a game to be heavy-duty work. Throughout the 1920s and 1930s, NFL teams tried other formations [most simply were variations on the Single Wing theme], but none caught on like the original Single Wing until the Bears destroyed the Redskins in 1940 using the T-Formation.)

The Los Angeles Rams got along well enough without the 11 players they traded to Dallas to go 9-3 and force a playoff game for the National Conference title with Detroit. But the resurging Lions beat the Rams, 31-21, in a fog-shrouded game at Detroit, then won their first NFL championship in 17 years by defeating the Browns 17-7. Quarterback Bobby Layne, halfback Doak Walker, and fullback Pat Harder starred on offense. Thus began a great era for the Lions under coach Buddy Parker (who played on Detroit's last championship team in 1935).

Baugh, whose slingshot sidearm delivery helped create the NFL's first precision passing attack, retired after playing his sixteenth season, the record at the time for NFL service. He still holds the records for most seasons leading the league in passing, six, and highest career punting average, 45.10 yards.

1952

AMERICAN CONFERENCE	W	L	T	Pct.	Pts.	OP
Cleveland	8	4	0	.667	310	213
N.Y. Giants	7	5	0	.583	234	231
Philadelphia	7	5	0	.583	252	271
Pittsburgh	5	7	0	.417	300	273
Chi. Cardinals	4	8	0	.333	172	221
Washington	4	8	0	.333	240	287

NATIONAL CONFERENCE	W	L	T	Pct.	Pts.	OP
Detroit	9	3	0	.750	344	192
Los Angeles	9	3	0	.750	349	234
San Francisco	7	5	0	.583	285	221
Green Bay	6	6	0	.500	295	312
Chi. Bears	5	7	0	.417	245	326
Dallas Texans	1	11	0	.083	182	427

National Conference playoff: DETROIT 31, Los Angeles 21
NFL championship: Detroit 17, CLEVELAND 7

team, named the Colts after the city's previous football franchise, entered the newly renamed Western Conference (formerly the National Conference). The American Conference was renamed Eastern Conference.

Three consecutive conference titles didn't prevent the Browns from being sold. Arthur McBride sold the Cleveland team to a syndicate headed by Dave R. Jones.

Otto Graham of the Browns was the league's top passer, Pete Pihos of the Eagles was the top receiver, and Joe Perry of the 49ers was the leading rusher. But the overall best team again was Detroit. The Lions proved it by winning the Western Conference and then, for the second year in a row, knocking off the Browns, 17-16, for the championship. Doak Walker scored 11 points and Bobby Layne passed 33 yards to end Jim Doran for the winning touchdown in the fourth quarter to delight a crowd of 54,577 in Briggs Stadium. It was an appropriate reward for the Motor City fans, who had supported the Lions throughout the season with an average attendance of 52,591.

The NFL policy of blacking out games in a team's home territory was challenged in court by the federal government, which contended it was a violation of antitrust laws. Judge Allan K. Grim of the U.S. District Court in Philadelphia upheld the blackout rule.

1953

EASTERN CONFERENCE

	W	L	T	Pct.	Pts.	OP
Cleveland	11	1	0	.917	348	162
Philadelphia	7	4	1	.636	352	215
Washington	6	5	1	.545	208	215
Pittsburgh	6	6	0	.500	211	263
N.Y. Giants	3	9	0	.250	179	277
Chi. Cardinals	1	10	1	.091	190	337

WESTERN CONFERENCE

	W	L	T	Pct.	Pts.	OP
Detroit	10	2	0	.833	271	205
San Francisco	9	3	0	.750	372	237
Los Angeles	8	3	1	.727	366	236
Chi. Bears	3	8	1	.273	218	262
Baltimore	3	9	0	.250	182	350
Green Bay	2	9	1	.182	200	338

NFL championship: DETROIT 17, Cleveland 16

1954

Roger Bannister of England broke the four-minute barrier in the mile run with a 3:59.4 clocking, and the Cleveland Browns broke the spell the Detroit Lions seemed to havc over them. The Browns won their fifth consecutive conference title since joining the NFL (their ninth in a row counting the AAFC years) and then blasted the defending champion Lions 56-10. Cleveland quarterback Otto Graham played avenger, scoring three touchdowns himself and passing for three more (two to Ray Renfro).

The season began with two important new contracts. Commissioner Bell was given a new 12-year contract and, in Baltimore, Weeb Ewbank was hired as head coach. Ewbank promised no miracles, but prophesied that it would take five years for his team to win the NFL championship.

NFL players also had a new contract with safety. It became practical for them to wear facemasks.

1954

EASTERN CONFERENCE

	W	L	T	Pct.	Pts.	OP
Cleveland	9	3	0	.750	336	162
Philadelphia	7	4	1	.636	284	230
N.Y. Giants	7	5	0	.583	293	184
Pittsburgh	5	7	0	.417	219	263
Washington	3	9	0	.250	207	432
Chi. Cardinals	2	10	0	.167	183	347

WESTERN CONFERENCE

	W	L	T	Pct.	Pts.	OP
Detroit	9	2	1	.818	337	189
Chi. Bears	8	4	0	.667	301	279
San Francisco	7	4	1	.636	313	251
Los Angeles	6	5	1	.545	314	285
Green Bay	4	8	0	.333	234	251
Baltimore	3	9	0	.250	131	279

NFL championship: CLEVELAND 56, Detroit 10

DEVELOPMENT OF THE UNIFORM

Y.A. Tittle, Quarterback, San Francisco 49ers *By the mid-1950s, the plastic helmet, with its web suspension, had become a league standard. Facemasks also gained in popularity, such as the lucite model Tittle wore, which gave way to single or dual bars.*

1955

The sudden-death overtime rule was invoked for the first time—on an experimental basis—when a preseason game between Los Angeles and New York in Portland, Oregon, ended in a tie. The Rams won 23-17 three minutes into overtime.

Dr. Jonas Salk developed a vaccine which would prevent polio, but in the NFL nobody could figure out a way to stop Paul Brown's Cleveland machine. The league's top passer, Otto Graham, playing in his last season, led the Browns to yet another conference title. He silenced 85,693 fans at the Los Angeles Coliseum by directing a 38-14 victory over the Rams in the NFL Championship Game. NBC paid $100,000 for the rights to televise the game, $25,000 more than the DuMont network had paid in 1951.

The season was one of budding hope in Baltimore. After going 3-9 each of their first two seasons, the Colts raised their record to 5-6-1. The nucleus of a contender was being formed; rookie fullback Alan (The Horse) Ameche led the league in rushing with 961 yards.

1955

EASTERN CONFERENCE

	W	L	T	Pct.	Pts.	OP
Cleveland	9	2	1	.818	349	218
Washington	8	4	0	.667	246	222
N.Y. Giants	6	5	1	.545	267	223
Chi. Cardinals	4	7	1	.364	224	252
Philadelphia	4	7	1	.364	248	231
Pittsburgh	4	8	0	.333	195	285

WESTERN CONFERENCE

	W	L	T	Pct.	Pts.	OP
Los Angeles	8	3	1	.727	260	231
Chi. Bears	8	4	0	.667	294	251
Green Bay	6	6	0	.500	258	276
Baltimore	5	6	1	.455	214	239
San Francisco	4	8	0	.333	216	298
Detroit	3	9	0	.250	230	275

NFL championship: Cleveland 38, LOS ANGELES 14

Alan (The Horse) Ameche led NFL rushers in his rookie year.

1956

This was not a year for the favorites. The USA lost its first Olympic Games since 1936, as measured by medal totals, to the Russians. George Halas retired as coach of the Bears, and was replaced by Paddy Driscoll. And the Browns failed to win a divisional championship for the first time since the formation of the team in 1946.

With Otto Graham gone, Cleveland foundered to fourth place in the Eastern Conference. The New York Giants rose to fill the vacuum. A full-scale rebuilding job overseen by coach Jim Lee Howell (ably assisted by Vince Lombardi and Tom Landry, among others) was completed.

The Giants, who had moved from the Polo Grounds to Yankee Stadium, won their first NFL title since 1938 by defeating the Chicago Bears 47-7 before a crowd of 56,836 in New York. The big guns for the Giants were quarterback Charlie Conerly, who passed for touchdowns to Kyle Rote and Frank Gifford, and runners Mel Triplett and Alex Webster, both of whom scored.

The game was played on an icy field and the Giants came out wearing sneakers just as they had in the second half of the famous ''Sneakers Game'' of 1934—and with the same result. There was one big difference, though. The players' shares for the championship game had risen significantly, to $3,779 for the winners and $2,485 for the losers.

As the Giants' rebuilding process reached its successful conclusion, the one in Baltimore continued. Seeking a backup for quarterback George Shaw, the Colts made an 80-cent phone call to a sandlot player named Johnny Unitas, and he joined the club. The lanky, crewcut, 22-year-old Unitas had been cut by the Steelers, who had drafted him in the ninth round out of Louisville.

Green Bay's Al Carmichael set an NFL record that never has been topped. He fielded a Chicago Bears kickoff in his own end zone and ran it back 106 yards for a touchdown.

Halfback Frank Gifford was an offensive giant for New York.

1956

EASTERN CONFERENCE	W	L	T	Pct.	Pts.	OP
N.Y. Giants	8	3	1	.727	264	197
Chi. Cardinals	7	5	0	.583	240	182
Washington	6	6	0	.500	183	225
Cleveland	5	7	0	.417	167	177
Pittsburgh	5	7	0	.417	217	250
Philadelphia	3	8	1	.273	143	215

WESTERN CONFERENCE	W	L	T	Pct.	Pts.	OP
Chi. Bears	9	2	1	.818	363	246
Detroit	9	3	0	.750	300	188
San Francisco	5	6	1	.455	233	284
Baltimore	5	7	0	.417	270	322
Green Bay	4	8	0	.333	264	342
Los Angeles	4	8	0	.333	291	307

NFL championship: N.Y. GIANTS 47, Chi. Bears 7

1957

The Russians got into the headlines by launching Sputnik I. On sports pages, the headlines were devoted to the San Francisco 49ers, who featured the looping, leaping "Alley Oop" passes of Y.A. Tittle to R.C. Owens, and the running of Hugh McElhenny and Joe Perry.

Emotion reached a peak in San Francisco when Tony Morabito, the club owner, collapsed and died during a game against Chicago in late October. Trailing 17-7 at the time, the 49ers fought back and got a bittersweet 21-17 victory on a fourth quarter pass from Tittle to end Billy Wilson. Coached by Frankie Albert, the spectacular and inventive 49ers were one of the league's hottest tickets. In November, a then league record crowd of 102,368 jammed the Los Angeles Coliseum to see the Rams defeat their intrastate archrivals 37-24.

The 8-4 49ers tied Detroit for the Western Conference title, forcing a playoff game for the right to meet Cleveland for the NFL championship. Cheered on by a capacity home crowd, the 49ers led 27-7 in the third quarter. But the Lions pulled off one of the most dramatic comebacks in NFL history, winning 31-27.

The championship game with Cleveland almost was anticlimatic. The Lions got revenge for their lopsided 1954 postseason loss by routing the Browns 59-14. Tobin Rote, filling in at quarterback for the injured Bobby Layne, threw four touchdown passes and scored one himself to help the Lions to their fourth NFL title.

Another California story with latent impact had been developing all season, but was eclipsed by the activity in San Francisco. Former Rams public relations director Pete Rozelle was named general manager of the team. The 31-year-old Rozelle, a native Californian, had fashioned a career for himself in sports public relations. He had gone from sports information director and assistant director of athletics in his senior year (1949) at the University of San Francisco to public relations director of the Rams in 1952. In January, 1955, he accepted an

DEVELOPMENT OF THE UNIFORM

Lenny Moore, Halfback, Baltimore Colts *The Colts' new uniform in 1957 featured horseshoe logos on the helmet and TV numbers on the shoulders of the nylon jersey. With mandatory taping of ankles, low-cut shoes replaced the old-fashioned high-tops.*

The 49ers' R.C. Owens alley-oops between two defenders.

offer to become the publicist for the 1956 Olympic Games in Melbourne, Australia. The next year he was back in Los Angeles and pro football.

1957

EASTERN CONFERENCE	W	L	T	Pct.	Pts.	OP
Cleveland	9	2	1	.818	269	172
N.Y. Giants	7	5	0	.583	254	211
Pittsburgh	6	6	0	.500	161	178
Washington	5	6	1	.455	251	230
Philadelphia	4	8	0	.333	173	230
Chi. Cardinals	3	9	0	.250	200	299

WESTERN CONFERENCE	W	L	T	Pct.	Pts.	OP
Detroit	8	4	0	.667	251	231
San Francisco	8	4	0	.667	260	264
Baltimore	7	5	0	.583	303	235
Los Angeles	6	6	0	.500	307	278
Chi. Bears	5	7	0	.417	203	211
Green Bay	3	9	0	.250	218	311

Western Conference playoff: Detroit 31, SAN FRANCISCO 27
NFL championship: DETROIT 59, Cleveland 14

1958

Chicago owner George Halas reinstated himself as coach of the Bears for the third time. The team's original coach from 1920 to 1929, Halas came back for stints from 1933 to 1942, and 1946 to 1955.

But it was another coach who proved to be the focus of NFL attention. True to his prediction, Weeb Ewbank brought Baltimore its first championship at the end of five years. With quarterback Johnny Unitas coolly directing the offense, the Colts won the Western Conference title with a 9-3 record, then waited for the outcome of the Eastern Conference playoff between Cleveland—who else?—and New York to determine their opponents in the NFL Championship Game. The Giants won 10-0, setting the stage for one of the pivotal games in league history.

Three days after Christmas, the Colts and Giants met in balmy (for December) 49-degree weather at Yankee Stadium. As a crowd of 64,185 (including 15,000 from Baltimore) watched, both teams did little but spar in the first quarter. Then Unitas took advantage of two fumbles by Frank Gifford, whom the Colts were keying on. Using Lenny Moore on sweeps, Alan Ameche up the middle, and short, finesse passes to end Raymond Berry, Unitas guided the Colts to a 14-3 halftime lead.

New York got inspired following a stirring third-quarter goal-line stand and, by the first minute of the fourth quarter, had taken a 17-14 lead on a pass from quarterback Charlie Conerly to Gifford. With the minutes ticking away, Gifford was stopped short on a controversial placement on third-and-four at the Giants' 40-yard line. Only 1:56 remained in the game, and the Giants punted.

The air was electric as the Colts took over and a cold, gray mist settled over the stadium. The Giants dropped into a prevent defense, wary of Unitas's long bombs to Moore. Taking advantage of the deep drops of the defensive backs, Unitas repeatedly threw underneath to

Colts quarterback Johnny Unitas, exhibits his cool in the 1958 NFL title game, called the "greatest game ever played."

Berry, driving the Colts to the New York 13 with 19 seconds left.

Out of time outs, the Baltimore field-goal unit ran on the field. Steve Myhra, who had made only 4 of 10 all season, kicked a 20-yard field goal with seven seconds on the clock to force the first sudden-death overtime in NFL championship history.

The Giants won the toss, but faltered on their first drive of the overtime. It would be their last. The Colts took over on their own 20 after New York's punt. From there, Unitas choreographed 13 plays that became part of football lore. At 8:15 of the overtime, Ameche slammed over from the 1 to give the Colts a 23-17 victory.

No game, before or since, created such an impact on the sport. Because of its dramatic nature, and the timing (the nation increasingly was turning to television for sports coverage), it was the game that put pro football on the map.

1958

EASTERN CONFERENCE	W	L	T	Pct.	Pts.	OP
N.Y. Giants	9	3	0	.750	246	183
Cleveland	9	3	0	.750	302	217
Pittsburgh	7	4	1	.636	261	230
Washington	4	7	1	.364	214	268
Chi. Cardinals	2	9	1	.182	261	356
Philadelphia	2	9	1	.182	235	306

WESTERN CONFERENCE	W	L	T	Pct.	Pts.	OP
Baltimore	9	3	0	.750	381	203
Chi. Bears	8	4	0	.667	298	230
Los Angeles	8	4	0	.667	344	278
San Francisco	6	6	0	.500	257	324
Detroit	4	7	1	.364	261	276
Green Bay	1	10	1	.091	193	382

Eastern Conference playoff: N.Y. GIANTS 10, Cleveland 0
NFL championship: Baltimore 23, N.Y. GIANTS 17, sudden death overtime

Charlton Heston arrived by chariot in the picture of the year, "Ben Hur," and won an Oscar as best actor. The NFL also saw the rise of two of its most mythic gladiators.

Vincent T. Lombardi did not ride into Green Bay, Wisconsin, in a chariot. By the time he departed as general manager in 1967, he could have been voted emperor of the north. Lombardi, the offensive coach of the Giants, left New York to take over the forlorn Packers. Green Bay had fallen on hard times. Its 1-10-1 record in 1958 was its poorest in 40 years, and its eleventh season in a row with a .500 or worse record. The 13-man committee that had been running the club had been rendered ineffectual by internal bickering.

"Let's get one thing straight," Lombardi announced upon arrival, "I'm in complete command around here." A martinet to some, an inspiration to others, Lombardi got immediate results. The Packers finished his first season with a 7-5 record.

In Cleveland, fullback Jim Brown was entering his third season. The Browns' number-one draft choice in 1957, the All-America from Syracuse led NFL rushers (as he did eight of his nine seasons) with 942 yards, and played in the first of his nine straight Pro Bowls. In 1958, he set an NFL record when he gained 1,527 yards rushing in a single season. By 1959, when he gained 1,329 yards, he had become the most feared runner in the NFL, and the standard against which all future rushers would be measured.

Even with Brown ruling the backfield, Cleveland finished second to New York (which still was mourning the loss in February of co-founder Tim Mara) in the Eastern Conference. Baltimore repeated in the Western Conference, setting up a championship game rematch in Baltimore. The two teams didn't reprise their memorable 1958 performance. The game remained close for three quarters. But in the final period, trailing 9-7, the Colts exploded for 24 consecutive points before the Giants

In his nine seasons, Jim Brown rewrote NFL rushing records.

could score again. Final: Baltimore 31, New York 16.

Familiar clouds had been forming on pro football's horizon since August, when Lamar Hunt had announced the formation of the American Football League. Old NFL hands knew a storm was on the way.

1959

EASTERN CONFERENCE	W	L	T	Pct.	Pts.	OP
N.Y. Giants	10	2	0	.833	284	170
Cleveland	7	5	0	.583	270	214
Philadelphia	7	5	0	.583	268	278
Pittsburgh	6	5	1	.545	257	216
Washington	3	9	0	.250	185	350
Chi. Cardinals	2	10	0	.167	234	324

WESTERN CONFERENCE	W	L	T	Pct.	Pts.	OP
Baltimore	9	3	0	.750	374	251
Chi. Bears	8	4	0	.667	252	196
Green Bay	7	5	0	.583	248	246
San Francisco	7	5	0	.583	255	237
Detroit	3	8	1	.273	203	275
Los Angeles	2	10	0	.167	242	315

NFL championship: BALTIMORE 31, N.Y. Giants 16

1960

You had to feel happy for the Philadelphia Eagles. Celebrating their victory in the NFL Championship Game, they hugged each other, mugged for photographers, tossed back their sweaty heads, and poured the sweet beverage of triumph into faces streaked with the mud of Franklin Field.

You had to feel happy for the Eagles, because it was the first chance they'd had for a decade. . .and the last they'd have for a couple more. After winning NFL titles in 1948 and 1949, they had spent the 1950s as also-rans, sometimes close but more often distant. After a 10-4 second-place finish in 1961, the Eagles struggled for most of the next 18 years, finally emerging in 1980 with an NFC championship and a trip to Super Bowl XV. But go back to the postgame revelry of 25 years ago. . . .

If a single player captured the spirit of the 1960 NFL Championship Game—and the pivotal quality of pro football in the early 1960s—it was Chuck Bednarik, the last of the 60-minute men, a combination center-linebacker.

Two years later, Bednarik would end his playing career. From then on, there were one-platoon guys. Sure, there were rarities during the next two decades. Roy Green, the defensive back the St. Louis Cardinals turned into an eventual league-leading wide receiver in 1980, was one. Green is versatile, but he never goes the full four quarters. For two-way, 60-minute men, Chuck Bednarik was it. From Bednarik on, pro football turned to specialization. Coaching staffs would grow to twice their 1960 size. Players' roles would refine themselves to undreamed-of precision as the game turned to finesse.

In the visitors' locker room at Franklin Field on that final day of the 1960 season, Packers head coach Vince Lombardi dealt with an emotion he'd be feeling for the last time: defeat in an NFL Championship Game. Lombardi's Green Bay teams of the 1960s would be NFL champions in 1961, 1962, 1965, 1966, and 1967, and in

The Eagles beat the Packers for the NFL Championship thanks to Chuck Bednarik's (60) game-saving tackle on the final play.

the latter two would graduate to a new level of competition, an event initially called the AFL-NFL World Championship Game by the league office. In the media, the games were known as Super Bowls I and II.

"AFL," of course, stood for American Football League. Born: 1960. Teams: Boston, Buffalo, Dallas, Denver, Houston, Los Angeles, New York, Oakland. Commissioner's resume: perfect. Joe Foss, a heavily decorated World War II fighter pilot and a national hero, chaired a group of owners that very early had dubbed itself "The Foolish Club."

While the new league's eight teams purchased uniforms and dived into the talent market for bodies to fill them, the NFL took on new leadership. Pete Rozelle, general manager and vice president of the Los Angeles Rams, was elected Commissioner. His charge: a league that since its founding in 1920 had evolved from 13 clubs to as many as 22, and after four decades, was back to 13, divided into two conferences.

Rozelle's predecessor was Bert Bell, a Main Line Philadelphia aristocrat whose death came at Franklin Field in 1959 as he watched the Eagles play the Pittsburgh Steelers from the end-zone stands.

The AFL's "Foolish Club": (standing, left to right) William H. Sullivan, Jr., Boston; Calvin W. Kunz, Jr., Denver; Ralph Wilson, Jr., Buffalo; Lamar Hunt, Dallas; Harry Wismer, New York; Wayne Valley, Oakland; Barron Hilton, Los Angeles; (seated) K.S. (Bud) Adams, Houston; and Joe Foss, Commissioner.

Rozelle's ascension at age 33 to what some considered an interim role as Commissioner came after an arduous 23-ballot selection meeting among the league's owners; he was a compromise candidate nominated to break a hopeless stalemate.

The NFL's modest expansion from 12 to 13 teams in

1960 was its first in 10 years. In 1950, it had absorbed the Cleveland Browns, San Francisco 49ers, and Baltimore Colts from the fallen, four-year-old All-America Football Conference.

The new team played in Dallas, wore blue stars on its white helmets and jersey shoulders, and called itself the Cowboys. Its head coach, Tom Landry, had been a player (mainly a defensive back) and a coaching colleague of Lombardi with the New York Giants, under Jim Lee Howell. (Another new NFL franchise, to be located in Minneapolis-St. Paul, was awarded in 1960 to be activated in 1961.)

Although the frustration of the Cowboys' early years would give rise to the familiar outcry for the coach's dismissal, Dallas owner Clint Murchison's response would be to provide a new 10-year contract for Landry. To this day, Landry is the only coach the Cowboys have known.

In its first game, played at the Cotton Bowl on September 29, Dallas got a 345-yard passing performance from diminutive Eddie LeBaron, the former Washington Redskins quarterback. But Pittsburgh quarterback and native Texan Bobby Layne threw four touchdown passes and kicked all five extra points as the Steelers defeated the Cowboys 35-28. The Cowboys, 0-11-1 in their first season, were NFL cellar material. Off the field they faced an AFL competitor, the Dallas Texans, at the box office. Likewise, the New York Giants and Los Angeles Rams found themselves "sharing" their cities' pro football marketplaces with the New York Titans and Los Angeles Chargers of the AFL.

The AFL immediately threw a new wrinkle into pro football's relationship with television, selling ABC the rights to its games for $2 million. In the unique package, the eight teams shared the revenue equally.

The AFL got its start on Friday night, September 9, at Boston University Field. Denver Broncos flanker Al Carmichael (formerly of Green Bay) caught a 59-yard pass from Frank Tripucka and scored the first touchdown in league history. Later, their teammate, Gene Mingo, returned a punt 76 yards for a touchdown, giving Denver a 13-10 victory over the Boston Patriots.

AFL founder Lamar Hunt's team, the Dallas Texans, was at the Los Angeles Coliseum the next evening to face Barron Hilton's Chargers, named after his newly initiated "Carte Blanche" credit card but symbolized by a white horse on the club's logo and lightning bolts on their helmets. Mixed metaphors and all, the Chargers defeated the Texans 21-20 as NFL castoff quarterback Jack Kemp passed for one touchdown and ran for another, both in the fourth quarter. (The Chargers' biggest asset probably was its coaching staff, headed by Sid Gillman, who lured a group of assistants whose names would became prominent during the next 24 years—Chuck Noll, Al Davis, Jack Faulkner, and Don Klosterman.)

The AFL completed its three-day grand opening on Sunday, September 11. At Kezar Stadium in San Francisco, Houston Oilers quarterback George Blanda, formerly of the Chicago Bears, threw four touchdown passes in a 37-22 victory over the Oakland Raiders, whose quarterback, rookie Tom Flores, completed only 13 of 32 passing attempts. At the Polo Grounds in New York, owner Harry Wismer's Titans spotted the Buffalo Bills a field goal in the first quarter, then held Buffalo quarterbacks Bob Brodhead and Tom O'Connell to 26 passing yards, winning 27-3.

When the Oilers had identified themselves as the class of the new league (their 6-3 record in late season belied their offensive might, and offense was the end-all in the early years of the AFL), the late Tex Maule wrote in *Sports Illustrated*: "The question is: how good are the Oilers (and, for that matter, how good is the rest of the league)? Unquestionably, the Oilers are better than Missouri or Minnesota or Mississippi. They are smarter and more versatile than these college teams; but they are not as good as the Dallas Cowboys, the newest and weakest team in the National Football League. The Cowboys, who are smarter and more versatile than the Oilers, would beat them, and easily."

The Oilers didn't have the Cowboys on their schedule in 1960, of course; the two teams wouldn't play a regular-season game until 1970. Tex Maule must have had at least a silent chuckle when the Cowboys won that one 52-10. But that's getting ahead of the story. In the first AFL Championship Game, against the Chargers, Houston's Blanda passed for 301 yards and three touchdowns. Oilers halfback Billy Cannon, the 1959 Heisman Trophy winner from LSU whose signing under the goal posts immediately following the Sugar Bowl had been an early AFL public relations coup, was the title game's most valuable player. His 88-yard touchdown reception from Blanda provided the decisive points as the Oilers defeated the Chargers 24-16.

Conversations around the hot stove burned into the night. NFL, AFL, what was your pleasure? Fun times lay ahead.

1960 NFL

EASTERN CONFERENCE

	W	L	T	Pct.	Pts.	OP
Philadelphia	10	2	0	.833	321	246
Cleveland	8	3	1	.727	362	217
N.Y. Giants	6	4	2	.600	271	261
St. Louis	6	5	1	.545	288	230
Pittsburgh	5	6	1	.455	240	275
Washington	1	9	2	.100	178	309

WESTERN CONFERENCE

	W	L	T	Pct.	Pts.	OP
Green Bay	8	4	0	.667	332	209
Detroit	7	5	0	.583	239	212
San Francisco	7	5	0	.583	208	205
Baltimore	6	6	0	.500	288	234
Chicago	5	6	1	.455	194	299
L.A. Rams	4	7	1	.364	265	297
Dall. Cowboys	0	11	1	.000	177	369

NFL championship: PHILADELPHIA 17, Green Bay 13

1960 AFL

EASTERN CONFERENCE

	W	L	T	Pct.	Pts.	OP
Houston	10	4	0	.714	379	285
N.Y. Titans	7	7	0	.500	382	399
Buffalo	5	8	1	.385	296	303
Boston	5	9	0	.357	286	349

WESTERN CONFERENCE

	W	L	T	Pct.	Pts.	OP
L.A. Chargers	10	4	0	.714	373	336
Dall. Texans	8	6	0	.571	362	253
Oakland	6	8	0	.429	319	388
Denver	4	9	1	.308	309	393

AFL championship: HOUSTON 24, L.A. Chargers 16

1961

Movement and change marked the early months of the AFL's second year, the NFL's forty-second.

San Diego got a franchise in the new league, as the Chargers moved south from Los Angeles. In the NFL, the Washington Redskins moved into newly constructed D.C. Stadium (later to be named in memory of slain presidential candidate Robert F. Kennedy). Art Modell purchased the Cleveland Browns. The San Francisco 49ers, enamored of their Shotgun formation and its prerequisite that a quarterback be able to run, traded Y.A. Tittle to the New York Giants for guard Lou Cordileone. The deal was a godsend for the Giants, as Tittle led them to three consecutive championship games.

The NFL got its fourteenth franchise with the birth of the Minnesota Vikings. The state's last NFL team had been the Minneapolis Red Jackets (1929-30), whose combined record of 2-16-1 netted them two next-to-last-place finishes.

Norm Van Brocklin, who had retired following his championship victory as the Philadelphia Eagles' quarterback, was the new club's head coach. The Vikings chose their first players as the Dallas Cowboys had—from a list submitted by the league's 13 other teams. But they had an advantage over the Cowboys; they also were able to take part in the annual college draft. Minnesota's draft class was headed by Tulane halfback Tommy Mason and Georgia quarterback Fran Tarkenton. Never one to avoid a macho challenge, Van Brocklin, the fiery "man's man" quarterback, subtly shifted gears and became Van Brocklin the drill sergeant, labeling his garage-sale bunch "the thirty-six stiffs."

In their maiden game, the "stiffs" upset Chicago 37-13. Tarkenton, whose serpentine scrambles in the seasons ahead would madden Van Brocklin as much as they enthralled spectators, passed for four touchdowns and ran for a fifth. The NFL didn't know it yet, but here was its inventive, improvising, can-do, overachieving

DEVELOPMENT OF THE UNIFORM

Paul Hornung, Halfback, Green Bay Packers *Equipment and padding became more specialized by player position and physical condition. The rollbar Hornung wore around his neck protected a pinched nerve by cushioning whiplash-type movements.*

quarterback for the 1960s and 1970s, inaugurating his career with a team that would win only 2 of its next 13 games.

While the Vikings struggled, the Green Bay Packers drove to an 11-3 record and a championship-game victory over the New York Giants. The 1961 title game represented the coronation of the Packers' dynasty. Lombardi's "run to daylight" theme was predicated on a swift, strong offensive line. At its core were guards Jerry Kramer and Fred (Fuzzy) Thurston, men who made daylight for fullback Jim Taylor and multi-purpose halfback Paul Hornung. Quarterback Bart Starr, reliable and serviceable and sometimes even spectacular, was in his sixth season, well-matured for the adventures ahead. Against the Giants on the last day of the year, Hornung set an NFL Championship Game record by scoring 19 points in a 37-0 rout.

Also notable in the statistical review of 1961 were the accomplishments of two players whose offensive prominence spanned, when combined, almost two decades: Cleveland fullback Jim Brown (1957-1965) and Philadelphia (and later Washington) quarterback Sonny Jurgensen (1957-1974). Brown, the league's leading rusher for the fifth time in his five-year career, tied his own single-game mark with 237 yards against the Eagles. Jurgensen set an NFL single-season record by passing for 3,723 yards.

The AFL style of play, meanwhile, got its "look" from the likes of Denver receiver Lionel Taylor, whose pro football-record 100 catches hid beneath his team's 3-11 showing. Just to show that this was a league that lived by the pass, Houston's George Blanda threw seven touchdown passes, tying a pro football record, in a 49-13 victory over the New York Titans. Then, just to show that this was a league that refused to be labeled easily, Blanda and the Oilers held off the transplanted Chargers for a 10-3 victory in the AFL Championship Game.

Mark 1961, too, as a memorable year in pro football's

successful marriage to television. The game had grown more and more salable to the major networks since the late 1950s, when the Baltimore Colts' sudden-death overtime victory against the New York Giants in the 1958 NFL Championship Game mesmerized millions tuned to the CBS telecast. Commissioner Rozelle, himself, challenged by the potential impact of television on his sport, began to lobby. So, in 1961, came Senator Emanuel Celler (D-New York) with a bill legalizing single-network package sales by professional sports leagues. President John F. Kennedy signed it into law; by January, 1962, the NFL and CBS had agreed on a two-year contract calling for total rights fees of $4,650,000 annually.

1961 NFL

EASTERN CONFERENCE	W	L	T	Pct.	Pts.	OP	WESTERN CONFERENCE	W	L	T	Pct.	Pts.	OP
N.Y. Giants	10	3	1	.769	368	220	Green Bay	11	3	0	.786	391	223
Philadelphia	10	4	0	.714	361	297	Detroit	8	5	1	.615	270	258
Cleveland	8	5	1	.615	319	270	Baltimore	8	6	0	.571	302	307
St. Louis	7	7	0	.500	279	267	Chicago Bears	8	6	0	.571	326	302
Pittsburgh	6	8	0	.429	295	287	San Francisco	7	6	1	.538	346	272
Dallas Cowboys	4	9	1	.308	236	380	Los Angeles	4	10	0	.286	263	333
Washington	1	12	1	.077	174	392	Minnesota	3	11	0	.214	285	407

NFL championship: GREEN BAY 37, N.Y. Giants 0

1961 AFL

EASTERN DIVISION	W	L	T	Pct.	Pts.	OP	WESTERN DIVISION	W	L	T	Pct.	Pts.	OP
Houston	10	3	1	.769	513	242	San Diego	12	2	0	.857	396	219
Boston Patriots	9	4	1	.692	413	313	Dallas Texans	6	8	0	.429	334	343
N.Y. Titans	7	7	0	.500	301	390	Denver	3	11	0	.214	251	432
Buffalo	6	8	0	.429	294	342	Oakland	2	12	0	.143	237	458

AFL championship: Houston 10, SAN DIEGO 3

1962

Head coach Jack Faulkner's idea of burning the Denver Broncos' ghastly, vertically-striped brown and yellow stockings at a public bonfire may have been as much witchcraft as it was public relations. The Broncos jumped from 3-11 to 7-7, good enough for a second-place Western Division finish in 1962. But Faulkner's magic extended to only two of the next 18 games, and the Broncos let him go after the first four games of 1964.

The Texans gave the city of Dallas a goodby gift in 1962, defeating Houston for the AFL title in sudden-death overtime before moving to Kansas City to become the Chiefs.

If the Oilers' habitual appearance in the AFL finale suggested stability, that notion was easily shaken by the reminder that they had done it under three different head coaches—Lou Rymkus, Wally Lemm, and Frank (Pop) Ivy. Before the decade was over, the team made three more coaching changes, switching to Sammy Baugh in 1964, Hugh (Bones) Taylor in 1965, and back to Lemm in 1966. An Oilers executive once left the following instructions with his secretary: "If the head coach calls while I'm out, be sure to get his name."

Nineteen-sixty-two also was the year the AFL got its first 1,000-yard rusher, Carlton (Cookie) Gilchrist of the Buffalo Bills. It was the first year in American pro football for the 6-foot 2-inch, 243-pound fullback, after eight seasons in the Canadian Football League.

Off the field, the AFL's charges of NFL monopoly and conspiracy—in the areas of expansion, television, and player signings—fell flat in a U.S. District Court. Competition for college talent tilted heavily in the NFL's favor at the outset of 1962.

NFL rules makers ordained that a 15-yard penalty would be assessed whenever a player tackled another by the facemask.

Green Bay repeated as NFL champion, powered by Jim Taylor's league-leading 1,474 yards rushing and an

Big Cookie Gilchrist was the AFL's first 1,000-yard rusher.

NFL-record 19 touchdowns. The former statistic grew in stature a few seasons later when it was noted that this was the only time Cleveland fullback Jim Brown had yielded the rushing title in his nine-year career.

In a wild shootout between two of the period's great quarterbacks, Y.A. Tittle threw a record-tying seven touchdowns as the New York Giants defeated the Washington Redskins and Sonny Jurgensen 49-34. Tittle's generation slipped a little further into the NFL's past with the retirements of Chuck Bednarik and Bobby Layne. There went the last of the two-way players and, in Layne's case, the last of the get-it-done-on-the-field-and-raise-hell-afterward quarterbacks. In fact, the most colorful of them all.

1962 NFL

EASTERN CONFERENCE	W	L	T	Pct.	Pts.	OP
N.Y. Giants	12	2	0	.857	398	283
Pittsburgh	9	5	0	.643	312	363
Cleveland	7	6	1	.538	291	257
Washington	5	7	2	.417	305	376
Dallas Cowboys	5	8	1	.385	398	402
St. Louis	4	9	1	.308	287	361
Philadelphia	3	10	1	.231	282	356

WESTERN CONFERENCE	W	L	T	Pct.	Pts.	OP
Green Bay	13	1	0	.929	415	148
Detroit	11	3	0	.786	315	177
Chicago	9	5	0	.643	321	287
Baltimore	7	7	0	.500	293	288
San Francisco	6	8	0	.429	282	331
Minnesota	2	11	1	.154	254	410
Los Angeles	[illegible]	[illegible]	1	.077	220	334

NFL championship: Green Bay 16, N.Y. GIANTS 7

1962 AFL

EASTERN DIVISION	W	L	T	Pct.	Pts.	OP
Houston	11	3	0	.786	387	270
Boston Patriots	9	4	1	.692	346	295
Buffalo	7	6	1	.538	309	272
N.Y. Titans	5	9	0	.357	278	423

WESTERN DIVISION	W	L	T	Pct.	Pts.	OP
Dallas Texans	11	3	0	.786	389	233
Denver	7	7	0	.500	353	334
San Diego	4	10	0	.286	314	392
Oakland	1	13	0	.071	213	370

AFL championship: Dallas Texans 20, HOUSTON 17, sudden death overtime

Defensive tackle Merlin Olsen (74) and end David (Deacon) Jones were the right side of the Rams' Fearsome Foursome line.

parlayed quarterback Tom Flores, center Jim Otto, receiver Art Powell, and league-leading rusher Clem Daniels into an attacking style that yielded a 10-4 record, one game behind eventual champion San Diego. (Flores, who later would take the Raiders to Super Bowl XV and XVIII victories as their head coach, had been a charter member of the team in 1960. After missing 1962 because of illness, he came on in 1963 to replace Davis's initial quarterback, Cotton Davidson.)

The era of Silver and Black, Pride and Poise, and Commitment to Excellence—catchwords used by the Raiders during the next two decades as they assembled professional sports' best overall record—had begun. If the NFL had struck a theme of assertiveness, the AFL had seen to it that the battle was more than joined.

1963 NFL

EASTERN CONFERENCE

	W	L	T	Pct.	Pts.	OP
N.Y. Giants	11	3	0	.786	448	280
Cleveland	10	4	0	.714	343	262
St. Louis	9	5	0	.643	341	283
Pittsburgh	7	4	3	.636	321	295
Dallas	4	10	0	.286	305	378
Washington	3	11	0	.214	279	398
Philadelphia	2	10	2	.167	242	381

WESTERN CONFERENCE

	W	L	T	Pct.	Pts.	OP
Chicago	11	1	2	.917	301	144
Green Bay	11	2	1	.846	369	206
Baltimore	8	6	0	.571	316	285
Detroit	5	8	1	.385	326	265
Minnesota	5	8	1	.385	309	390
Los Angeles	5	9	0	.357	210	350
San Francisco	2	12	0	.143	198	391

NFL championship: CHICAGO 14, N.Y. Giants 10

1963 AFL

EASTERN DIVISION

	W	L	T	Pct.	Pts.	OP
Boston Patriots	7	6	1	.538	327	257
Buffalo	7	6	1	.538	304	291
Houston	6	8	0	.429	302	372
N.Y. Jets	5	8	1	.385	249	399

WESTERN DIVISION

	W	L	T	Pct.	Pts.	OP
San Diego	11	3	0	.786	399	255
Oakland	10	4	0	.714	363	282
Kansas City	5	7	2	.417	347	263
Denver	2	11	1	.154	301	473

Eastern Division playoff: Boston 26, BUFFALO 8
AFL championship: SAN DIEGO 51, Boston 10

1964

America's rival pro football leagues were having some fun now, and if you didn't believe it, you could check the windows up and down the block on Sunday afternoons for television's unmistakable, bluish glow. The NFL's new, bigger-than-ever, two-year deal with CBS, consummated after a cloak-and-dagger, sealed-bid auction among the three major networks, meant more than $1 million a year for each team, an unheard-of sum. Meanwhile, Sonny Werblin orchestrated a five-year package for the AFL with rejected NFL suitor NBC that assured each team roughly $900,000 a year. "That does it," said Pittsburgh Steelers owner Art Rooney. "They no longer have to address us as 'Mister.' "

Television provided another new twist, this one the technical brainchild of CBS director Tony Verna. He had introduced it, actually, during the 1963 Army-Navy game. After Army's Rollie Stichweh ran for a touchdown late in the game, viewers were treated to a second showing of the play. *Instant replay!* At last, television had lifted the penalty for going to the refrigerator.

CBS's new toy came along just in time to review a play that Minnesota defensive end Jim Marshall probably wished never had been seen the first time. Houston writer Mickey Herskowitz recalled the episode years later in *PRO!* magazine:

"...yet, despite his greater achievements, Marshall always will be remembered around the NFL as Wrong Way Marshall. In 1964, he scooped up a fumble in San Francisco, carried it 66 yards into the end zone, and then joyfully flung the ball toward the stands. It was the lineman's dream come true. Alas, he had run into the wrong end zone for a safety. He sensed something was wrong when the 49ers began to congratulate him.

"Later, a booster club in Dallas honored Marshall with its Bonehead of the Year Award. He caught the wrong plane and flew to the wrong city—but it was all part of the act."

Marshall played on, and retired at age 41 in possession of a record that may never be broken, 282 consecutive games over a 19-year career. He was part of the Purple People Eaters, Minnesota's answer to the Rams' Fearsome Foursome. The other Eaters were tackles Alan Page and Gary Larsen and end Carl Eller.

In the mercurial AFL, Sonny Werblin's upgrading of the Jets took the team to multi-purpose Shea Stadium, situated in the midst of the recent New York World's Fair in Flushing Meadow, Queens. The move signaled a succession of similar transfers, taking pro football out of such aging venues as San Francisco's Kezar Stadium, home of the 49ers from 1946-1970 and the Oakland Raiders in 1960-61. (The Raiders' early odyssey took them from Kezar to Candlestick Park and eventually to Oakland's Frank Youell Field, a municipal sandlot exposed to the treacherous Nimitz Freeway, prior to their arrival at the new Oakland-Alameda County Coliseum in 1966.)

Houston's George Blanda attempted a record 505 passes in 1964 (68 of them in a loss to Buffalo), and end Charley Hennigan caught 101 of them for another record. The Oilers, however, slipped to 4-10, poorest in the Eastern Division. Buffalo (12-2) defeated San Diego (8-5-1) in the AFL Championship Game, 20-7.

Power shifted radically in the NFL's Eastern Division, as the New York Giants, about to bid farewell to two honored veterans, quarterback Y.A. Tittle and defensive end Andy Robustelli, sank to a 2-10-2 last-place finish. Cleveland, flourishing under the coaching of Blanton Collier, the passing of Frank Ryan to rookie split end Paul Warfield and flanker Gary Collins, and Jim Brown's seventh rushing title in eight years—went 10-3-1 for first. Western Division champion Baltimore, led by the passing of quarterback Johnny Unitas and an NFL-record 20 touchdowns by halfback-flanker Lenny Moore, was heavily favored in the title game. But Ryan, comfortable in cold and windy Cleveland Stadium, came out after a scoreless first half and threw three touch-

DEVELOPMENT OF THE UNIFORM

Bob Lilly, Defensive Tackle, Dallas Cowboys *Dallas' ultra modern jersey was made of nylon with satin numerals. The pants were a metallic knit of polyurethane material. Lilly's plastic helmet featured a tubular steel and plastic ''bird cage'' facemask.*

down passes to Collins. The Browns scored a 27-0 upset, earning the largest winners' shares to date, $8,052 per man.

Unitas was the NFL's most valuable player in 1964, in the midst of a career that still ranks as the finest ever among professional quarterbacks. In 1956, the Pittsburgh Steelers had drafted him in the ninth round, out of Louisville. "Too dumb," Steelers coach Walt Kiesling told owner Art Rooney in training camp. The Browns gave Unitas a look, too, and told him to wait a year. So he took a job as the "monkey," or high man, on a pile driver setting the foundations for a tinning mill in Aliquippa, Pennsylvania. He was playing sandlot football for $6 a game when the Colts telephoned and invited him for a tryout. (The cost of the call was 80 cents, although NFL folklore at one time had it down to about a quarter.)

Unitas was not physically imposing. His shoulders slouched, and his marble-white skin covered a lean, almost gaunt frame. Could this physique be equipped with history's best passing mechanism?

He had many gifts. He had a deceptive delivery. He was the master of looking one way, staring down a cornerback, and throwing somewhere else. His arm put the ball where he wanted it to go, especially when he wanted it to go deep, with almost inhuman consistency.

Raymond Berry, Unitas's favorite receiver and still fourth on the all-time NFL list with 631 catches, once said, "I'm not sure he ever had a bad game. Maybe he had a bad half."

But the quality that made Unitas the complete quarterbacking package was his leadership.

"John would sometimes make calls in games against us that just didn't make any sense at all," said Los Angeles Rams defensive tackle Merlin Olsen. "But everybody on his team believed they were brilliant calls, and they made the plays work. So they became brilliant calls. Another quarterback could have called the same plays and ten guys would have looked at him like he was from Mars. And the plays wouldn't have worked."

In the context of the rivalry between the NFL and AFL, Unitas alone sometimes was suggested as the difference between the two leagues. "No, we don't have Johnny Unitas," said Lou Saban, head coach of the AFL's Buffalo Bills, "but there are thirteen teams in the National Football League that don't have him, either."

The Steelers, whose rejection of Unitas was just one of many regrets, finished 1964 with a 5-9 record, not far ahead of the slumbering Giants. But the Steelers had a running back whose accomplishments have weathered time's abrasions on the record book. In 1964, John Henry Johnson's contribution to the NFL was a total of 1,048 yards rushing. He was 35 at the time.

1964 NFL

EASTERN CONFERENCE

	W	L	T	Pct.	Pts.	OP
Cleveland	10	3	1	.769	415	293
St. Louis	9	3	2	.750	357	331
Philadelphia	6	8	0	.429	312	313
Washington	6	8	0	.429	307	305
Dallas	5	8	1	.385	250	289
Pittsburgh	5	9	0	.357	253	315
N.Y. Giants	2	10	2	.167	241	399

WESTERN CONFERENCE

	W	L	T	Pct.	Pts.	OP
Baltimore	12	2	0	.857	428	225
Green Bay	8	5	1	.615	342	245
Minnesota	8	5	1	.615	355	296
Detroit	7	5	2	.583	280	260
Los Angeles	5	7	2	.417	283	339
Chicago	5	9	0	.357	260	379
San Francisco	4	10	0	.286	236	330

NFL championship: CLEVELAND 27, Baltimore 0

1964 AFL

EASTERN DIVISION

	W	L	T	Pct.	Pts.	OP
Buffalo	12	2	0	.857	400	242
Boston Patriots	10	3	1	.769	365	297
N.Y. Jets	5	8	1	.385	278	315
Houston	4	10	0	.286	310	355

WESTERN DIVISION

	W	L	T	Pct.	Pts.	OP
San Diego	8	5	1	.615	341	300
Kansas City	7	7	0	.500	366	306
Oakland	5	7	2	.417	303	350
Denver	2	11	1	.154	240	438

AFL championship: BUFFALO 20, San Diego 7

1965

The NFL could point proudly to a class of rookies that included halfback Gale Sayers and linebacker Dick Butkus of Chicago, flanker-kick returner Bob Hayes of Dallas, and running back Ken Willard of San Francisco. Sayers highlighted his first season by tying an NFL record with six touchdowns in the Bears' 61-20 rout of the 49ers on a rain-soaked field in Chicago.

The center of attention, however, was an AFL rookie: Alabama quarterback Joe Namath, who signed with Sonny Werblin's New York Jets for more than $400,000. By outbidding the St. Louis Cardinals, who refused to offer Namath a no-cut contract, the Jets landed the most publicized blow in the six-year interleague rivalry.

The NFL's off-the-field highlight was a new television contract with CBS that called for $18.8 million a year, plus $2 million for the championship game. In the league expansion "game," the score was 1-1, as the NFL announced plans to add a franchise in Atlanta, the AFL in Miami.

For the second straight year, Buffalo dominated San Diego in winning the AFL Championship Game, this time 23-0. The Chargers' Paul Lowe, who had led the AFL with 1,121 yards in the regular season, was limited to 57 by Bills head coach Lou Saban's tough defense.

In the NFL, Jim Brown's ninth and final season ended with another rushing title (1,544 yards), and Cleveland again won the Eastern Division. But there were audible tremors coming from Dallas. The Cowboys finished second at 7-7 with help from Olympic 100-meter champion Bob Hayes at flanker, quarterback Don Meredith's 22 touchdown passes, and computer-advised "sleeper" draftees such as defensive tackle Jethro Pugh from Elizabeth City (North Carolina) State, an eleventh-round choice.

Western Division champion Green Bay held Brown to 50 yards in chilly weather, and on a muddy field that had to be cleared with shovels and snow plows, the

Gale Sayers, the Chicago Bears' record-setting rookie rusher.

Packers scored a 23-12 victory for their third NFL championship of the decade. Paul Hornung, finishing his second season since being reinstated from his 1963 gambling suspension (Detroit's Alex Karras also was reinstated after a year's exile), rushed for 105 yards and was supported by Jim Taylor's 96.

Green Bay and Baltimore had tied for the Western Division championship with 10-3-1 records. The Packers won the playoff 13:39 into sudden-death overtime on a field goal by Don Chandler. Both teams played that day with substitute quarterbacks. The Packers' Zeke Bratkowski filled in for Bart Starr, who was hurt on the game's first play, while Tom Matte, a halfback who had played quarterback at Ohio State, directed the Colts. Johnny Unitas and Gary Cuozzo, Baltimore's starting and second-string quarterbacks, were injured and unable to play the Colts' regular-season finale against Los Angeles. While Green Bay was being tied by San Francisco, Matte started against the Rams and, wearing a wristband equipped with a list of plays, led the Colts to a 20-17 victory. He led all rushers that day with 99 yards, and set up the winning field goal.

1965 NFL

EASTERN CONFERENCE

	W	L	T	Pct.	Pts.	OP
Cleveland	11	3	0	.786	363	325
Dallas	7	7	0	.500	325	280
N.Y. Giants	7	7	0	.500	270	338
Washington	6	8	0	.429	257	301
Philadelphia	5	9	0	.357	363	359
St. Louis	5	9	0	.357	296	309
Pittsburgh	2	12	0	.143	202	397

WESTERN CONFERENCE

	W	L	T	Pct.	Pts.	OP
Green Bay	10	3	1	.769	316	224
Baltimore	10	3	1	.769	389	284
Chicago	9	5	0	.643	409	275
San Francisco	7	6	1	.538	421	402
Minnesota	7	7	0	.500	383	403
Detroit	6	7	1	.462	257	295
Los Angeles	4	10	0	.286	269	328

Western Conference playoff: GREEN BAY 13, Baltimore 10, sudden death overtime
NFL championship: GREEN BAY 23, Cleveland 12

1965 AFL

EASTERN DIVISION

	W	L	T	Pct.	Pts.	OP
Buffalo	10	3	1	.769	313	226
N.Y. Jets	5	8	1	.385	285	303
Boston Patriots	4	8	2	.333	244	302
Houston	4	10	0	.286	298	429

WESTERN DIVISION

	W	L	T	Pct.	Pts.	OP
San Diego	9	2	3	.818	340	227
Oakland	8	5	1	.615	298	239
Kansas City	7	5	2	.583	322	285
Denver	4	10	0	.286	303	392

AFL championship: Buffalo 23, SAN DIEGO 0

1966

A voice came from the heavens. "Tell Nobis to sign with the Oilers," said orbiting astronaut Frank Borman. It was Borman's way of rooting for the AFL team in its bid to sign 1966's hottest college prospect, linebacker Tommy Nobis of Texas.

The Oilers almost pulled it off. But after putting Houston management on hold with the old "give us a day to think it over" routine, Nobis's agent put the last commas and zeroes on the linebacker's contract with the newly formed Atlanta Falcons of the NFL.

Score another for the senior circuit, and watch the temperature rise.

Meanwhile, voices closer to the ground than Borman's were beginning to ask more and more seriously: Why fight? Why not join?

"After the 1965 season I was convinced the structure of pro football was in trouble," said Dallas Cowboys president-general manager Tex Schramm in a 1984 interview, "because teams in both leagues were no longer drafting the best players. The draft became predicated on which players you could sign. In our league two or three teams were signing all their players—the Rams, the Cowboys, and the Packers. There were a few in the AFL—the Chiefs, the Jets, and the Raiders. Many of the other teams couldn't compete. Boston was drafting players who should have been third- or fourth-round picks in the first round because they thought they could sign them. And there was a lot of switching around of draft choices. It was just getting to be insane." (In fact, so certain were the AFL teams that Heisman Trophy winner Mike Garrett of USC would sign with the Rams, that none even bothered to draft him until the Chiefs did in the twentieth round, eventually signing him.)

On April 6, 1966, Schramm met Kansas City owner Lamar Hunt near the Texas Ranger statue at Love Field Airport in Dallas. The topics: detente and a possible merger.

The two sat in Schramm's car in the airport parking lot. "I told him that this was not just conversation," Schramm said, "that Pete Rozelle knew about it and approved. But I explained that only a few of our owners were aware of it and suggested that he keep it as confidential as possible for a while. Pro football owners are individualists and competitors who like to compete in public. At this stage, twenty-four owners would have made the discussions too unwieldy, so I suggested to Lamar that I be his only direct contact in the NFL, and he would be mine in the AFL."

Two days later, at a meeting in Houston, Al Davis was elected to replace Joe Foss as commissioner of the AFL. Foss had been criticized by some of the owners for being an absentee commissioner. Davis, persuaded by Hunt, San Diego's Sid Gillman, and other AFL leaders to take the job, would say later, "I guess they thought I'd be a catalyst. It was a situation that called for some constant pressure to be put on the other side."

So went the odd scenario, with Hunt and Schramm

NFL Commissioner Pete Rozelle presents Vince Lombardi with the World Championship trophy, later named for the coach.

quietly plotting an armistice and Davis polishing his brass knuckles. The situation exploded when New York Giants owner Wellington Mara signed Pete Gogolak, a Hungarian-born placekicker (pro football's first "soccer" stylist) who had played out his option with Buffalo of the AFL.

Until that point, the two leagues, despite their dueling for college talent, had refrained from signing each other's veteran players. All attention had been directed to the pursuit of college talent, as evidenced by the league's combined $7 million outlay for 1966 draft choices (Green Bay alone spent $1 million for running backs Donny Anderson and Jim Grabowski, neither of whom immediately would be a regular starter). Now, by signing Gogolak, Mara had broken into the demilitarized zone, as it were.

Davis came out swinging. He recruited Houston general manager Don Klosterman and Oakland general manager Scotty Stirling. Their mission: Go after the NFL's star players—especially the quarterbacks—and spare no expense.

Klosterman and Oilers owner Bud Adams offered San Francisco 49ers quarterback John Brodie $750,000 over 10 years. Chicago Bears tight end Mike Ditka signed with the Oilers for a $50,000 bonus. Stirling signed Los Angeles Rams quarterback Roman Gabriel with a reported $100,000 down payment. All this six-figure activity aroused interest among other NFL stars, including quarterbacks Sonny Jurgensen of Washington, Fran Tarkenton of Minnesota, and Milt Plum of Detroit. Davis admitted contacting Green Bay defensive backs Willie Wood and Herb Adderley and steering them toward Jets owner Sonny Werblin. George Wilson, head coach of the AFL's new Miami franchise, was rumored to be talking contract with Detroit tackle Alex Karras.

Whether these player-contract talks served as a stimulus or hindrance to a possible merger is debatable. But Schramm and Hunt quickened the pace of their merger discussions. On May 31, Hunt went to Schramm's home in Dallas and went over the formal merger proposal. Hunt took down all of Schramm's provisions on a legal-sized yellow notepad. Schramm said, "There it is. If you accept, this deal has been approved by every NFL club. If you have to alter it too much, it will blow up."

A week later, after Hunt had had time to run the details past AFL owners and Rozelle had been rounding up pro-merger votes (especially from skeptics such as Mara and 49ers president Lou Spadia), all was in readiness. The merger was announced June 8 at a press conference at the Warwick Hotel in New York.

Highlights of the announced agreement included:

—a world championship game between the two leagues, beginning at the end of the 1966 season;

—a common draft, with the first scheduled for January, 1967;

—preseason interleague play beginning in 1967;

—a single NFL regular-season schedule beginning in 1970;

—an $18-million indemnity to be paid by the AFL to the NFL over 20 years;

—two expansion franchises to be added by 1968, one in each league;

—no relocation of existing clubs.

Pete Rozelle would be the commissioner.

John Brodie would be rich.

San Francisco retained rights to Brodie as specified by the merger agreement, but he still had a valuable napkin. On it was written the agreement he had reached with Klosterman and the Oilers.

"Somebody owes me $750,000," Brodie said. A month later, a deal was struck guaranteeing him a minimum of $921,000 over 12 years, plus legal fees. The 49ers agreed to pay more than half the figure, and the other 23 teams (from both leagues) contributed equal shares to settle the difference. Gabriel and Ditka got their money too, but the main news was an end to the big bonus outlays.

On October 21, Congress passed special legislation

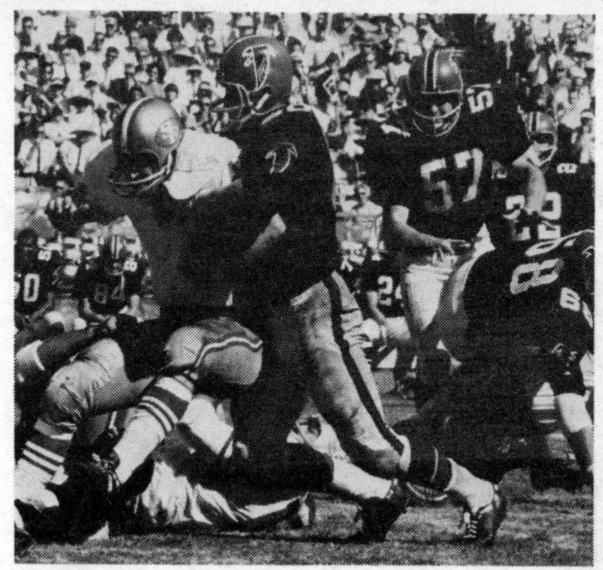

Linebacker Tommy Nobis starred in Atlanta's first NFL season.

exempting the merger agreement from United States antitrust laws.

Atlanta, the NFL's fifteenth team, was placed in the Eastern Conference and finished 3-11, avoiding last place thanks to the New York Giants' 1-12-1 showing.

This also was the inaugural year for the Miami Dolphins of the AFL. In their first game, running back Joe Auer returned the opening kickoff 95 yards for a touchdown, but Oakland spoiled the party 23-14.

Two teams headed for no particular distinction in the year's Eastern Conference standings, Washington and the New York Giants, gained special distinction November 27 at D.C. Stadium by playing the highest-scoring game in NFL history. The Redskins won 72-41.

The Dallas Cowboys "arrived" in the seventh year of their existence, becoming the first expansion team in history to win a division or conference title. They took their 10-3-1 record against Green Bay (12-2) in the NFL

Championship Game and gave the Packers a good scare. The Cowboys reached the Green Bay 2-yard line late in the game, when Don Meredith, hit hard by linebacker Dave Robinson, managed to get a pass away, only to have it intercepted by Tom Brown in the end zone. Green Bay held on 34-27.

The Kansas City Chiefs—coached by Hank Stram, quarterbacked by Len Dawson and fortified on defense by tackle Buck Buchanan and linebacker Bobby Bell—defeated the Buffalo Bills 31-7 for the AFL title, earning the right to meet Vince Lombardi's Packers in the first AFL-NFL World Championship Game.

The contest was telecast by both CBS and NBC and was blacked out in Los Angeles. It was not a sellout, drawing 63,035 to the Los Angeles Memorial Coliseum, which could hold 98,000. The Packers took a 14-10 halftime lead and drew away early in the second half when Willie Wood's 50-yard interception return set up a touchdown by halfback Elijah Pitts. Quarterback Bart Starr threw two touchdown passes to Max McGee and was voted the game's most valuable player.

With the presence of teams from both leagues on the same field, pro football had entered a new era.

1966 NFL

EASTERN CONFERENCE

	W	L	T	Pct.	Pts.	OP
Dallas	10	3	1	.769	445	239
Cleveland	9	5	0	.643	403	259
Philadelphia	9	5	0	.643	326	340
St. Louis	8	5	1	.615	264	265
Washington	7	7	0	.500	351	355
Pittsburgh	5	8	1	.385	316	347
Atlanta	3	11	0	.214	204	437
N.Y. Giants	1	12	1	.077	263	501

WESTERN CONFERENCE

	W	L	T	Pct.	Pts.	OP
Green Bay	12	2	0	.857	335	163
Baltimore	9	5	0	.643	314	226
Los Angeles	8	6	0	.571	289	212
San Francisco	6	6	2	.500	320	325
Chicago	5	7	2	.417	234	272
Detroit	4	9	1	.308	206	317
Minnesota	4	9	1	.308	292	304

NFL championship: Green Bay 34, DALLAS 27

Super Bowl I: Green Bay (NFL) 35, Kansas City (AFL) 10, at Memorial Coliseum, Los Angeles, Calif.

1966 AFL

EASTERN DIVISION

	W	L	T	Pct.	Pts.	OP
Buffalo	9	4	1	.692	358	255
Boston Patriots	8	4	2	.677	315	283
N.Y. Jets	6	6	2	.500	322	312
Houston	3	11	0	.214	335	396
Miami	3	11	0	.214	213	362

WESTERN DIVISION

	W	L	T	Pct.	Pts.	OP
Kansas City	11	2	1	.846	448	276
Oakland	8	5	1	.615	315	288
San Diego	7	6	1	.538	335	284
Denver	4	10	0	.286	196	381

AFL championship: Kansas City 31, BUFFALO 7

1967

How many NFL fans still can name the four "C's"? The Capitol and Century divisions of the Eastern Conference and the Central and Coastal divisions of the Western Conference would be the league's competitive framework for the years 1967-69.

In the first common draft combining teams from the AFL and NFL, Baltimore used the first choice to take Michigan State defensive end Bubba Smith. The Colts had traded with newcomer New Orleans, whose debut at Tulane Stadium under head coach Tom Fears began Dolphins-style. Echoing the feat of Joe Auer, Saints rookie John Gilliam took the opening kickoff 94 yards for a touchdown. The opponent was Fears's former team, the Los Angeles Rams, who came back to win 27-13. The Saints won only 3 of 14 that year.

Another "first" had entered the record books when an NFL team, Detroit, met an AFL team, Denver, in a preseason game at Denver's Bears Stadium. The Broncos became the first AFL team to defeat an NFL team. The date was August 5. The score was 13-7.

Placekickers everywhere joined fans of the St. Louis Cardinals in a standing ovation when the team defeated Pittsburgh 28-14. Why this unique union of supporters? Jim Bakken accounted for all the points the Cardinals would need, kicking a record seven field goals.

For the fourth and last time, George Halas removed himself from the head-coaching job of the team he owned, the Chicago Bears, finishing the season with a 7-6-1 record, second-best in the Central Division behind Green Bay. The Packers, who seemed to have reached their competitive apogee in early November with a 55-7 trouncing of Cleveland in what was billed as the match-up of the year, went on to knock over the red-hot Los Angeles Rams 28-7 in the first round of the playoffs, then defeated Dallas 21-17 for the NFL title, in a game that has become known as the Ice Bowl.

In the AFL, the individual accomplishment of 1967

belonged to New York Jets quarterback Joe Namath, whose record 4,007 yards passing and 26 touchdowns still did not translate to a league—or even a division—championship. The Jets (8-5-1) lost out to Houston (9-4-1), and the Oilers went on to play doormat to Oakland, losing to the Raiders 40-7 in the AFL Championship Game.

The Oilers had released 39-year-old George Blanda, and the Raiders had signed him as a free agent. Blanda spent the year as Oakland's kicker and a backup to quarterback Daryle Lamonica, who also was a find for Oakland. After spending four years in Buffalo, Lamonica joined the Raiders in 1967, led the AFL in passing, and was named the league's most valuable player.

In the second AFL-NFL World Championship Game, played at Miami's Orange Bowl, the Packers got four field goals from Don Chandler and easily defeated the Raiders 33-14. Two weeks later, it was announced that Vince Lombardi had resigned as Green Bay's head coach. Lombardi would take over as the Packers' general manager, and assistant Phil Bengtson would take his place. "Take his place" was a figure of speech.

The New Orleans Saints began play in the new Capitol Division.

In 12-below-zero weather, Bart Starr's (15) late quarterback sneak behind guard Jerry Kramer helped Green Bay win the Ice Bowl.

1967 NFL

EASTERN CONFERENCE

Capitol Division

	W	L	T	Pct.	Pts.	OP
Dallas	9	5	0	.643	342	268
Philadelphia	6	7	1	.462	351	409
Washington	5	6	3	.455	347	353
New Orleans	3	11	0	.214	233	379

Century Division

	W	L	T	Pct.	Pts.	OP
Cleveland	9	5	0	.643	334	297
N.Y. Giants	7	7	0	.500	369	379
St. Louis	6	7	1	.462	333	356
Pittsburgh	4	9	1	.308	281	320

WESTERN CONFERENCE

Coastal Division

	W	L	T	Pct.	Pts.	OP
Los Angeles	11	1	2	.917	398	196
Baltimore	11	1	2	.917	394	198
San Francisco	7	7	0	.500	273	337
Atlanta	1	12	1	.077	175	422

Central Division

	W	L	T	Pct.	Pts.	OP
Green Bay	9	4	1	.692	332	209
Chicago	7	6	1	.538	239	218
Detroit	5	7	2	.417	260	259
Minnesota	3	8	3	.273	233	294

Los Angeles won division title on the basis of advantage in points (58-34) in two games vs. Baltimore.

Conference championships: DALLAS 52, Cleveland 14; GREEN BAY 28, Los Angeles 7

NFL championship: GREEN BAY 21, Dallas 17

Super Bowl II: Green Bay (NFL) 33, Oakland (AFL) 14, at Orange Bowl, Miami, Fla.

1967 AFL

EASTERN DIVISION

	W	L	T	Pct.	Pts.	OP
Houston	9	4	1	.692	258	199
N.Y. Jets	8	5	1	.615	371	329
Buffalo	4	10	0	.286	237	285
Miami	4	10	0	.286	219	407
Boston Patriots	3	10	1	.231	280	389

WESTERN DIVISION

	W	L	T	Pct.	Pts.	OP
Oakland	13	1	0	.929	468	233
Kansas City	9	5	0	.643	408	254
San Diego	8	5	1	.615	360	352
Denver	3	11	0	.214	256	409

AFL championship: OAKLAND 40, Houston 7

1968

If social change in America reached its full 50-state boiling point in 1968, pro football shared part of the front burner. One labor agreement—between the AFL and its players association—was reached, while similar talks in the NFL screeched to a halt, then lunged to settlement a few days before training camps opened. The football world was sure to change, too, with the return of Paul Brown as part-owner and head coach of this year's expansion team, the Cincinnati Bengals of the AFL.

This was the year of the "Heidi Game," the Raiders' 43-32 victory over the New York Jets at Oakland. Denied the last two minutes of the telecast when it was preempted by the movie "Heidi," fans went crazy.

This also was the year the Houston Oilers moved from Rice Stadium to the Astrodome, a.k.a. the Great Indoors, a.k.a. the Eighth Wonder of the World. Also the home of baseball's Astros, it was America's first domed stadium, the first to use AstroTurf (what else?), the first to have luxury suites, and the first to have an animated scoreboard. Houston's Bud Adams, now the owner of the NFL's first team to air-condition its home games (the thermostat was set at 72 degrees), would say years later, "If the Astrodome is the Eighth Wonder of the World, the rent is the Ninth."

Meanwhile, there was a new order in New York, as Sonny Werblin sold the Jets to four partners. One of them, Don Lillis, became head of the corporation. When Lillis died two months later, Phil Iselin was named president of the club. The Jets finished the season 11-3, champions of the AFL's Eastern Division by a four-game margin over Houston. When the Jets avenged their "Heidi Game" loss with a 27-23 victory over Oakland in the AFL Championship Game at Shea Stadium, head coach Weeb Ewbank became the first coach ever to win titles in both the NFL and the AFL.

Ewbank had coached the Baltimore Colts to the NFL championship in 1958, the storied sudden-death over-

Quarterback Joe Namath and fullback Matt Snell were the main offensive weapons in the Jets' Super Bowl III upset victory.

time victory with its final drive steered by Johnny Unitas in the early winter darkness at Yankee Stadium. Unitas to Raymond Berry. Unitas to Jim Mutscheller. Unitas giving to Alan Ameche, through a hole opened by Mutscheller, George Preas, and Lenny Moore. . .and into an empty end zone. Ewbank was there.

Now he was headed for Miami and Super Bowl III, the first of the series to take the name. The heavily favored NFL champion Colts no sooner had arrived in town when they began hearing their supremacy challenged by the upstart pretenders from the "other league." The high point came at a media breakfast during Super Bowl week, when quarterback Joe Namath gave his "guarantee" that the Jets would win on Sunday. They did, 16-7.

The Colts team that lost to the Jets that day was coached by Don Shula, who had the use of an older and more brittle Unitas—to open the season, that is. When Unitas went out with an elbow injury, Shula replaced him with Earl Morrall. The former Michigan State star threw 26 touchdown passes, and the Colts went 13-1 before beating Minnesota (which had won its first Central Division title) 24-14 for the championship of the Western Conference. The Browns, winners of the Century Division after a quarterback switch of their own (Bill Nelsen replacing Frank Ryan), beat Capitol Division winner Dallas but were no match for the Colts in the NFL Championship Game. The Colts won 34-0 as Tom Matte scored three touchdowns.

Even before the season had begun, a record of sorts fell to a team that had been doing its share for a number of years in the talent department—the University of Southern California Trojans. Since 1968, no school has been as highly represented in the first round of the draft. Five USC players were among the first 24 chosen: tackle Ron Yary (first to Minnesota), tackle Mike Taylor (tenth to Pittsburgh), defensive end Tim Rossovich (fourteenth to Philadelphia), running back Mike Hull (sixteenth to Chicago), and wide receiver Earl McCullouch (twenty-fourth to Detroit).

Rookie running back Paul Robinson led all AFL rushers in 1968, the inaugural season of the expansion Cincinnati Bengals.

1968 NFL

EASTERN CONFERENCE

Capitol Division

	W	L	T	Pct.	Pts.	OP
Dallas	12	2	0	.857	431	186
N.Y. Giants	7	7	0	.500	294	325
Washington	5	9	0	.357	249	358
Philadelphia	2	12	0	.143	202	351

Century Division

	W	L	T	Pct.	Pts.	OP
Cleveland	10	4	0	.714	394	273
St. Louis	9	4	1	.692	325	289
New Orleans	4	9	1	.308	246	327
Pittsburgh	2	11	1	.154	244	397

WESTERN CONFERENCE

Coastal Division

	W	L	T	Pct.	Pts.	OP
Baltimore	13	1	0	.929	402	144
Los Angeles	10	3	1	.769	312	200
San Francisco	7	6	1	.538	303	310
Atlanta	2	12	0	.143	170	389

Central Division

	W	L	T	Pct.	Pts.	OP
Minnesota	8	6	0	.571	282	242
Chicago	7	7	0	.500	250	333
Green Bay	6	7	1	.462	281	227
Detroit	4	8	2	.333	207	241

Conference championships: CLEVELAND 31, Dallas 20; BALTIMORE 24, Minnesota 14
NFL championship: Baltimore 34, CLEVELAND 0
Super Bowl III: N.Y. Jets (AFL) 16, Baltimore (NFL) 7, at Orange Bowl, Miami, Fla.

1968 AFL

EASTERN DIVISION

	W	L	T	Pct.	Pts.	OP
N.Y. Jets	11	3	0	.786	419	280
Houston	7	7	0	.500	303	248
Miami	5	8	1	.385	276	355
Boston Patriots	4	10	0	.286	229	406
Buffalo	1	12	1	.077	199	367

WESTERN DIVISION

	W	L	T	Pct.	Pts.	OP
Oakland	12	2	0	.857	453	233
Kansas City	12	2	0	.857	371	170
San Diego	9	5	0	.643	382	310
Denver	5	9	0	.357	255	404
Cincinnati	3	11	0	.214	215	329

Western Division playoff: OAKLAND 41, Kansas City 6
AFL championship: N.Y. JETS 27, Oakland 23

1969

A meeting of NFL and AFL owners took almost 36 consecutive hours to come up with it, but the restructured NFL arrived on the scene May 17. Two 13-team conferences were formed by joining three teams from the previous NFL—Baltimore, Cleveland, and Pittsburgh—with the 10 teams from the AFL. The new amalgam was called the American Football Conference (AFC), and the remaining 13 teams made up the new National Football Conference (NFC). Each Conference would include three divisions—East, Central, and West.

The common draft among all 26 teams was a common occurrence by now, but what made it uncommon in 1969 was the presence of O.J. Simpson, USC's Heisman Trophy running back, who was drafted by Buffalo. Two more players whose careers would unfold to Hall-of-Fame dimensions, linebacker Ted Hendricks of Miami and defensive tackle Joe Greene of North Texas State, were taken by Baltimore and Pittsburgh, respectively.

Greene was the first draft choice of new head coach Chuck Noll, a former guard and linebacker with the Cleveland Browns (1953-59) and later an AFL and NFL assistant. Noll served as Don Shula's defensive backfield coach at Baltimore before accepting the Steelers' offer. In Noll's first season as head coach, the Steelers won their first game, then lost their last 13. By the time the 1979 season was over, they would be four-time Super Bowl champions.

For some NFL teams, getting ready for the 1969 season, let alone a dynasty, was enough of a production in itself.

The Oakland Raiders, like Pittsburgh, got a new head coach, former assistant John Madden. Unlike Noll, Madden was expected to maintain a winning tradition. He would respond with 112 victories in a 10-year career, including a 32-14 triumph over Minnesota in Super Bowl XI. Madden left coaching after the 1978 season and

Tough guy quarterback Joe Kapp led Minnesota to Super Bowl IV.

eventually became CBS's most popular football analyst, combining his knowledge of the game with a folksy, let's-get-acquainted repartee that was fine-tuned in the Amtrak club cars he chose over jetliners. Madden also became a familiar figure in television commercials, syndicated a radio broadcast, and wrote numerous articles on the game for the NFL's *PRO!* magazine. His 1984 collaboration with Dave Anderson, *Hey, Wait a Minute! I Wrote a Book,* was a mainstay on the best-seller lists throughout the football season.

This was the year the Washington Redskins got the services of an NFL legend and lost a legendary former owner. Vince Lombardi became part-owner, executive vice president, and head coach of the Redskins in February, and in August, George Preston Marshall died at age 72.

Marshall, who owned the team since its infancy in Boston, never was known for his mild demeanor. . .or for making himself obscure. One of the game's master pitchmen, he fielded pro football's first marching band (complete with its team's own fight song) and set up a radio network that carried the Redskins' games throughout the South. Marshall was responsible for major competitive changes in the 1930s, including a set schedule, divisional playoffs, moving the goal posts to the goal lines, and redesigning the ball in a narrower shape to encourage more forward passing. He also was the last owner to integrate his team when, in 1962, he traded for Cleveland halfback Bobby Mitchell. (With the draft choice they received in exchange for Mitchell, the Browns selected Syracuse's Ernie Davis, and were planning to team him with Jim Brown in a dream backfield. Davis never played professional football. He died of leukemia in 1963.)

In Los Angeles, owner Dan Reeves reluctantly recanted when his players protested the firing of head coach George Allen, and the Rams' troubled ship rocked to an 11-3 record, comfortably ahead of Coastal Division runner-up Baltimore, mortal again (8-5-1) in its post-Super Bowl slide.

Teams of the NFL wore a patch in the shape and design of the league's trademark shield, with the numeral "50" stitched prominently to commemorate the fiftieth anniversary of the league's founding in a Canton, Ohio, automobile showroom in 1920.

The New Orleans Saints, who had won three games in their initial season of 1967 and four in 1968, stuck to their pattern by winning five in 1969. One of those victories, a 51-42 offensive field day against St. Louis, put Saints quarterback Billy Kilmer and Cardinals quarterback Charley Johnson in the record book for the highest total of touchdown passes in one game, 12. Saints wide receiver Danny Abramowicz led the NFL with 73

DEVELOPMENT OF THE UNIFORM

Buck Buchanan, Defensive Tackle, Kansas City Chiefs *The AFL-NFL merger had an effect on uniforms, as did increased television coverage. In 1970 a league rule was adopted requiring all players' names to appear on the backs of their jerseys.*

catches. The highlight film ended about there, as the Saints, like the Cardinals, finished third in their division.

The AFL's leading receiver for the second straight year, Lance Alworth of San Diego, completed a string of 96 consecutive games with at least one reception—a record Abramowicz would break five years later after being traded to San Francisco. Alworth, eventually inducted into the Pro Football Hall of Fame in 1978 (and the first AFL player to be so honored), teamed with John Hadl in coach Sid Gillman's pass-oriented system. They nicknamed Alworth "Bambi," after Walt Disney's fawn, for his youthful features and the leaping grace of his receiving style.

San Diego's Gillman was forced to resign after nine games. Assistant Charlie Waller took over, and the Chargers finished off the pace, third in the AFL's Western Division at 8-6.

The 1969 AFL playoff structure took a new turn. Instead of playing within their divisions in the opening round, teams crisscrossed, with the Eastern Division champion Jets (10-4) playing Western Division runner-up Kansas City (11-3), and Oakland (12-1-1) meeting Houston (6-6-2) in the other postseason opener.

The latter game proved to be the mismatch the experts expected. Raiders quarterback Daryle Lamonica, who had thrown 34 touchdown passes during the regular season, got six more against the Oilers, and Oakland breezed 56-7. In cold, windy Shea Stadium, Kansas City defeated the Jets 13-6, moving 80 yards in two plays to score the only touchdown of the day, a 19-yard pass from Len Dawson to Gloster Richardson.

The last AFL Championship Game was tied 7-7 midway through the third quarter at Oakland when Dawson, on third-and-14, scrambled out of trouble in his end zone and completed a 35-yard pass to Otis Taylor. That began a 98-yard drive to a go-ahead touchdown. The Chiefs eventually won 17-7, turning the ball over three times inside their own 30 in the fourth quarter but intercepting Lamonica (who had returned to the game with a jammed throwing hand) three times during that span, as well.

The NFL playoff picture was dominated by a purple haze, as the Minnesota Vikings became the first expansion team to win the league championship. They did it behind the macho-gritty leadership of quarterback Joe Kapp, down from eight seasons in the Canadian Football League and given to lumbering rollouts and a just-get-it-there passing style. Kapp led a come-from-behind drive that defeated Los Angeles in the first round of the playoffs on an icy field in Minnesota.

The Cleveland Browns came to the title game via a mud-soaked 38-14 playoff victory over Dallas. Kapp welcomed them to sunny, but freezing, Metropolitan Stadium in Bloomington with a 14-point first quarter: his 7-yard touchdown run and a 75-yard scoring pass to Gene Washington. It was 24-0 Vikings at the half and 27-7 at the end.

Kansas City never trailed the heavily favored Vikings in Super Bowl IV in New Orleans. The Chiefs drove to field goals of 48, 32, and 25 yards by Jan Stenerud on their first three possessions, then took a 16-0 lead at intermission when Mike Garrett ran five yards for a touchdown with 5:34 remaining in the half. The Vikings' comeback attempt drew them to 16-7 when Dave Osborn scored on a four-yard run with 4:32 left in the third quarter. Then, starting from his own 18, Dawson led a drive that ended when, from the Vikings' 46, he hit wide receiver Taylor with a short pass. Taylor ran through cornerback Earsell Mackbee, then effectively faked safety Karl Kassulke at the 10 before scoring the clincher. The Chiefs evened the score between the AFL and NFL at two Super Bowls apiece, winning 23-7.

During the game, NFL Films had put a microphone on Chiefs head coach Hank Stram, and the results were as enjoyable as his team's artistry against the Vikings. "Let's put out that fire, Leonard," the highlight film records Stram telling Dawson as Kansas City begins its insurance drive. "Let's matriculate that ball down the

Wide receiver Lance Alworth of San Diego, nicknamed "Bambi," eventually became the first AFL player in the Hall of Fame.

field,'' Stram shouts to his players as the drive continues.

Stram's showmanship and knack for concise explanations of the game's finer points, like John Madden's, later paid off in his radio and television commentary for CBS. NFL Films, meanwhile, had been functioning as a subsidiary of the league since 1964. The relationship had begun in 1962 when Blair Productions in Philadelphia, under the direction of Ed Sabol (soon to be joined by his son Steve), had contracted to film the Green Bay-New York Giants NFL Championship Game.

Since 1964, NFL Films has become the largest 16-millimeter film company in the world, winning 33 Emmy Awards for cinematography, editing, writing, producing, directing, and music. ''We came at a time when there was a crest at both ends—football and television,'' said Steve Sabol, who became the company's executive vice president in 1972. ''We straddled the wave.''

Television waves would reach network viewers in the early 1970s via all three major networks. After being turned down by CBS and NBC because their evening prime-time schedules already were set (and successful), the NFL turned to ABC, which was lagging in the ratings race, for a Monday-night package of 13 games. On Sundays, CBS would carry the NFC and NBC the AFC, with Super Bowl coverage alternating between those two networks (a pattern that eventually would be broken by ABC's coverage of Super Bowl XIX).

The rivalry between the two competing leagues during the 1960s helped stir interest in pro football. Under one flag, the clubs would discover even greater prosperity in the 1970s.

More than anything else, it was Pete Rozelle's Midas touch with television that sent the NFL's popularity soaring. Rozelle's artistry with the law of supply and demand, and his proficiency in the mazes of network politics and Madison Avenue advertising agencies, continually got results.

''He's always known how to operate in that jungle,''

said Cleveland owner Art Modell, once a television and advertising executive. "I know the jungle. I came out of it."

Noting that more than 60 million viewers had watched Super Bowl IV, Rozelle shed a little perspective on the NFL-television relationship. "When you realize that more people can watch a game on television in one afternoon than see the sport in person over a five-year period," he said, "you begin to understand the impact of television in creating widespread interest."

1969 NFL

EASTERN CONFERENCE

Capitol Division

	W	L	T	Pct.	Pts.	OP
Dallas	11	2	1	.846	369	223
Washington	7	5	2	.583	307	319
New Orleans	5	9	0	.357	311	393
Philadelphia	4	9	1	.308	279	377

Century Division

	W	L	T	Pct.	Pts.	OP
Cleveland	10	3	1	.769	351	300
N.Y. Giants	6	8	0	.429	264	298
St. Louis	4	9	1	.308	314	389
Pittsburgh	1	13	0	.071	218	404

WESTERN CONFERENCE

Coastal Division

	W	L	T	Pct.	Pts.	OP
Los Angeles	11	3	0	.786	320	243
Baltimore	8	5	1	.615	279	268
Atlanta	6	8	0	.429	276	268
San Francisco	4	8	2	.333	277	319

Central Division

	W	L	T	Pct.	Pts.	OP
Minnesota	12	2	0	.857	379	133
Detroit	9	4	1	.692	259	188
Green Bay	8	6	0	.571	269	221
Chicago	1	13	0	.071	210	339

Conference championships: Cleveland 38, DALLAS 14; MINNESOTA 23, Los Angeles 20

NFL championship: MINNESOTA 27, Cleveland 7

Super Bowl IV: Kansas City (AFL) 23, Minnesota (NFL) 7, at Tulane Stadium, New Orleans, La.

1969 AFL

EASTERN DIVISION

	W	L	T	Pct.	Pts.	OP
N.Y. Jets	10	4	0	.714	353	269
Houston	6	6	2	.500	278	279
Boston Patriots	4	10	0	.286	266	316
Buffalo	4	10	0	.286	230	359
Miami	3	10	1	.231	233	332

WESTERN DIVISION

	W	L	T	Pct.	Pts.	OP
Oakland	12	1	1	.923	377	242
Kansas City	11	3	0	.786	359	177
San Diego	8	6	0	.571	288	276
Denver	5	8	1	.385	297	344
Cincinnati	4	9	1	.308	280	367

Divisional Playoffs: Kansas City 13, N.Y. JETS 6; OAKLAND 56, Houston 7

AFL championship: Kansas City 17, OAKLAND 7

Joe Scarpati didn't receive any special awards at the end of the 1970 NFL season, but he did play a vital role in the first year of the new, fully merged NFL.

Kneeling 63 yards away from a goal post at Tulane Stadium, Scarpati took a snap from center, gingerly holding the football as if it were 1970's own italicized exclamation point. Then New Orleans kicker Tom Dempsey came through with that ferocious hammer of a shoe he wore—a prosthetic device on a foot deformed at birth—and sent the NFL's longest field goal flying.

It came on the last play of a November 8 game to beat Detroit 19-17. It was the high point of Dempsey's career, which would end in 1978 with the Buffalo Bills, after a round of short stops in Philadelphia, Los Angeles, and Houston. Dempsey was traveling the road of the conventional, i.e., straight-on, placekicker, a species endangered by a steady influx of soccer-style sidewinders.

Lest 1970 be thought of as Dempsey's year, there was another conventional-style kicker, one who doubled as a back-up quarterback, one whose *succession* of miracle endings has no special category in the record book, just an indelible mark in football's memory bank. Oakland's George Blanda, coming on for injured Daryle Lamonica at age 43, rescued the Raiders from apparent defeat five straight times. Two touchdown passes in a victory against Pittsburgh started the chain. The second project, a 48-yard field goal with three seconds to play, gave the Raiders a 17-17 tie with Kansas City. Next came a 52-yard field goal to beat Cleveland 23-20, again with three seconds to play, followed by a winning touchdown drive to beat Denver 24-19 and another field goal, this one with four seconds left, to beat San Diego 20-17.

The Browns had played the part of victors in another historical sidebar to the merger year by defeating the New York Jets 31-21 in the first episode of "ABC Monday Night Football." The new series featured the play-by-play of Keith Jackson, lighthearted banter from former Cowboys quarterback Don Meredith, and the high-sounding, pedantic verbiage of Howard Cosell. (In 1971, Jackson would be replaced by former New York Giants halfback-receiver Frank Gifford; later color commentators would include Alex Karras, Fran Tarkenton, and O.J. Simpson.)

Getting things in place for the 1970 season took some doing. With the makeup of the AFC already decided, the structure of the NFC's three divisions went through months of discussions. Five plans were submitted. The version drawn, lottery-style, by Commissioner Pete Rozelle, is the one in use today (with Tampa Bay added to the NFC's Central Division and Seattle to the AFC's Western Division).

Two remarkably similar stadiums located 260 miles from each other on the Ohio River—Riverfront in Cincinnati and Three Rivers in Pittsburgh—opened as homes of the Bengals and Steelers, as well as baseball's Reds and Pirates. Both circular, they had almost identical seating capacities (59,754 at Riverfront, 59,000 at Three Rivers) and had their playing surfaces covered with artificial turf in the new tradition of attempting to defy the elements.

Quarterback Terry Bradshaw of Louisiana Tech, the first pick of the NFL draft, joined the Steelers, another step toward the team's impending dominance of pro football in the 1970s.

Another power center was taking shape in Miami, as Dolphins owner Joe Robbie hired head coach Don Shula away from Baltimore. It took some intervention by Commissioner Rozelle to settle charges of tampering voiced by Baltimore owner Carroll Rosenbloom. Rozelle found that Robbie had indeed fouled the process by communicating with Shula through Rosenbloom's son Steve (a Colts administrative aide) while the owner was on an Asian vacation. Rozelle compensated the Colts for their loss with a first-round draft choice in 1971 (North Carolina running back Don McCauley). Baltimore's new head coach was Don McCafferty, one of Shula's assistants from 1963-69.

Shula would take the Dolphins to Super Bowl VI the following season, but this year McCafferty took the Colts to Super Bowl V. Baltimore's NFC opponent was the Dallas Cowboys, better known at this point in NFL history as "The Team That Couldn't Win the Big One" than as "America's Team" (a label they eventually received from NFL Films when it came time to title their 1977 highlight film).

Pete Rozelle remained Commissioner of the post-merger NFL.

Oakland's George Blanda became a hero to middle-aged jocks.

Dallas's losses to Green Bay in the 1966 and 1967 NFL Championship Games and to Cleveland in the 1968 and 1969 Eastern Conference Championship Games—despite being heavily favored in the latter two—earned them another sobriquet: ''Next Year's Champions.''

In 1970, ''Next Year'' looked as if it had come when Dallas (10-4) won the NFC's Eastern Division, defeated Detroit 5-0 in a divisional playoff game, and beat San Francisco 17-10 in the NFC Championship Game at Kezar Stadium to earn its first Super Bowl appearance.

Super Bowl V is remembered as the Blooper Bowl because of its 11 turnovers (7 by the Colts) and 14 penalties (9 by Dallas).

With less than two minutes to play and the score tied 13-13, the Cowboys began a drive for what could have been the winning score. But quarterback Craig Morton's high pass to halfback Dan Reeves bounced out of Reeves's hands at the Dallas 41 and into the grasp of Colts linebacker Mike Curtis, who returned it to the 28.

Then, with just five seconds left, rookie Jim O'Brien kicked a 32-yard field goal to give the Colts a 16-13 victory. The Cowboys had been denied again.

In keeping with the realignment, the new AFC-NFC Pro Bowl picked up where a varied tradition of postseason all-star games had left off. The series had begun in 1939 when the New York Giants defeated a team called the "Pro All-Stars," 13-10, at a minor-league baseball park in Los Angeles, Wrigley Field. The game evolved into an East-West event played annually in the Los Angeles Coliseum. The new AFC-NFC version would travel to various NFL cities during the 1970s, then move to Honolulu in 1980 for an extended run at Aloha Stadium.

1970

AMERICAN CONFERENCE

EASTERN DIVISION

	W	L	T	Pct.	Pts.	OP
Baltimore	11	2	1	.846	321	234
Miami*	10	4	0	.714	297	228
N.Y. Jets	4	10	0	.286	255	286
Buffalo	3	10	1	.231	204	337
Boston Patriots	2	12	0	.143	149	361

CENTRAL DIVISION

	W	L	T	Pct.	Pts.	OP
Cincinnati	8	6	0	.571	312	255
Cleveland	7	7	0	.500	286	265
Pittsburgh	5	9	0	.357	210	272
Houston	3	10	1	.231	217	352

WESTERN DIVISION

	W	L	T	Pct.	Pts.	OP
Oakland	8	4	2	.667	300	293
Kansas City	7	5	2	.583	272	244
San Diego	5	6	3	.455	282	278
Denver	5	8	1	.385	253	264

NATIONAL CONFERENCE

EASTERN DIVISION

	W	L	T	Pct.	Pts.	OP
Dallas	10	4	0	.714	299	221
N.Y. Giants	9	5	0	.643	301	270
St. Louis	8	5	1	.615	325	228
Washington	6	8	0	.429	297	314
Philadelphia	3	10	1	.231	241	332

CENTRAL DIVISION

	W	L	T	Pct.	Pts.	OP
Minnesota	12	2	0	.857	335	143
Detroit*	10	4	0	.714	347	202
Chicago	6	8	0	.429	256	261
Green Bay	6	8	0	.429	196	293

WESTERN DIVISION

	W	L	T	Pct.	Pts.	OP
San Francisco	10	3	1	.769	352	267
Los Angeles	9	4	1	.692	325	202
Atlanta	4	8	2	.333	206	261
New Orleans	2	11	1	.154	172	347

**Wild Card qualifier for playoffs*

Divisional playoffs: BALTIMORE 17, Cincinnati 0; OAKLAND 21, Miami 14
AFC championship: BALTIMORE 27, Oakland 17
Divisional playoffs: DALLAS 5, Detroit 0; San Francisco 17, MINNESOTA 14
NFC championship: Dallas 17, SAN FRANCISCO 10
Super Bowl V: Baltimore (AFC) 16, Dallas (NFC) 13, at Orange Bowl, Miami, Fla.

1971

Time and tide wait for no man, says the cliche, so George Allen decided to go the other way. "The future is now," he said, taking over as head coach of the Washington Redskins and immediately trading for veteran defensive players such as tackle Diron Talbert and linebackers Myron Pottios, Maxie Baughan, and Jack Pardee of the Rams. In doing so, he mortgaged the future of the franchise, giving up draft choices scheduled well into the 1970s.

Led by aging quarterback Billy Kilmer and running back Larry Brown, the Redskins finished second to Dallas in the NFL's Eastern Division, earning the wild-card playoff berth (the team's first playoff appearance since 1945), then proved that the future still was the future by losing to Western Division-champion San Francisco 24-20 in the playoff opener. The 49ers, finishing their first season in Candlestick Park, lost the NFC Championship Game to Dallas, and the Cowboys prepared to meet AFC champion Miami.

The Dolphins' Super Bowl VI appearance was a first for the young franchise. After 10 victories in the regular season, Miami opened the playoffs with a 27-24 double-overtime win over Kansas City in the longest NFL game ever played, then beat wild-card entry Baltimore 21-0 in the AFC Championship Game.

President Richard Nixon, a Dolphins constituent by virtue of his vacation residence in Key Biscayne, Florida, felt obligated to help coach Don Shula prepare for the game. "I think you can hit [wide receiver Paul] Warfield on that down-and-in pattern," the nation's chief executive told the coach. Warfield caught four passes; Dallas won 24-3.

The year had begun with an influx of new quarterbacks and new venues around the league. The Patriots expanded their territory, changing from "Boston" to "New England" and moving into brand-new 61,275-seat Schaefer Stadium in suburban Foxboro, Massachu-

Ever-poised Dallas Cowboys quarterback Roger Staubach.

Howard Cosell, Don Meredith, and Frank Gifford manned the mikes for the second season of ABC's Monday Night Football.

setts. Their housewarming introduced Jim Plunkett, thc 1970 Heisman Trophy-winning quarterback from Stanford. In the NFL draft, New Orleans had picked up the theme by taking Mississippi's Archie Manning, and Houston had doubled the ante by drafting Santa Clara's Dan Pastorini in the first round and Kansas State's Lynn Dickey in the third. (Plunkett, Manning, and Pastorini were the first three draft choices overall.)

Two games from the regular season would live on, not only in the memories of those who saw them, but under the "variety show" category in NFL Films's rich archives. In October, Detroit defeated Atlanta 41-38. Ten touchdowns were scored in the game, in five different ways: rushing, passing, a fumble recovery, a kickoff return, and the return of a blocked punt. Six weeks later, Washington led Chicago 15-9 until the Bears' Cyril Pinder scored on a 40-yard run in the fourth quarter. Chicago got its winning point when holder Bobby Douglass recovered an errant snap on the point-after attempt and threw a 30-yard pass to Dick Butkus, normally a linebacker, who was an eligible receiver on the play.

Four more teams changed home stadiums: Dallas, from the Cotton Bowl to Texas Stadium in suburban Irving; Philadelphia, from Franklin Field to Veterans Stadium; San Francisco, from Kezar Stadium to Candlestick Park; and Chicago, from Wrigley Field to Soldier Field. All but the last could be called "modernizing." The Bears had been denizens of Wrigley (nee Cubs Park) since changing their identity from the Decatur Staleys in 1921. They now occupied the league's oldest structure, built in 1924.

1971

AMERICAN CONFERENCE

EASTERN DIVISION	W	L	T	Pct.	Pts.	OP
Miami	10	3	1	.769	315	174
Baltimore*	10	4	0	.714	313	140
New England	6	8	0	.429	238	325
N.Y. Jets	6	8	0	.429	212	299
Buffalo	1	13	0	.071	184	394
CENTRAL DIVISION	**W**	**L**	**T**	**Pct.**	**Pts.**	**OP**
Cleveland	9	5	0	.643	285	273
Pittsburgh	6	8	0	.429	246	292
Houston	4	9	1	.308	251	330
Cincinnati	4	10	0	.286	284	265
WESTERN DIVISION	**W**	**L**	**T**	**Pct.**	**Pts.**	**OP**
Kansas City	10	3	1	.769	302	208
Oakland	8	4	2	.667	344	278
San Diego	6	8	0	.429	311	341
Denver	4	9	1	.308	203	275

NATIONAL CONFERENCE

EASTERN DIVISION	W	L	T	Pct.	Pts.	OP
Dallas	11	3	0	.786	406	222
Washington*	9	4	1	.692	276	190
Philadelphia	6	7	1	.462	221	302
St. Louis	4	9	1	.308	231	279
N.Y. Giants	4	10	0	.286	228	362
CENTRAL DIVISION	**W**	**L**	**T**	**Pct.**	**Pts.**	**OP**
Minnesota	11	3	0	.786	245	139
Detroit	7	6	1	.538	341	286
Chicago	6	8	0	.429	185	276
Green Bay	4	8	2	.333	274	298
WESTERN DIVISION	**W**	**L**	**T**	**Pct.**	**Pts.**	**OP**
San Francisco	9	5	0	.643	300	216
Los Angeles	8	5	1	.615	313	260
Atlanta	7	6	1	.538	274	277
New Orleans	4	8	2	.333	266	347

**Wild Card qualifier for playoffs*

Divisional playoffs: Miami 27, KANSAS CITY 24, sudden death overtime; Baltimore 20, CLEVELAND 3

AFC championship: MIAMI 21, Baltimore 0

Divisional playoffs: Dallas 20, MINNESOTA 12; SAN FRANCISCO 24, Washington 20

NFC championship: DALLAS 14, San Francisco 3

Super Bowl VI: Dallas (NFC) 24, Miami (AFC) 3, at Tulane Stadium, New Orleans, La.

1972

A year of oddities got started when two men agreed to trade their NFL franchises. Illinois businessman Robert Irsay, who had purchased the Los Angeles Rams from the estate of the late Dan Reeves, swapped with Carroll Rosenbloom, owner of the Baltimore Colts. Neither team's performance on the field matched the excitement of the trade; each finished third in its division.

No, the thrills were in Miami, where the Miami Dolphins fashioned the NFL's first and only perfect season (17-0). En route to their 14-7 victory over Washington in Super Bowl VII, they nearly were derailed by Pittsburgh in the AFC Championship Game, surviving 21-17.

The Steelers had reached the AFC's final round by virtue of Franco Harris's "Immaculate Reception" a week earlier against Oakland. Pittsburgh's 13-7 triumph at Three Rivers Stadium was the front end of a cross-country "Black Saturday" for both San Francisco Bay Area teams. The 49ers suffered a last-minute catastrophe of their own, as Dallas's Roger Staubach threw two touchdown passes in 38 seconds to give the Cowboys, the NFC wild-card entry, a 30-28 victory.

Statistically, the New York Jets' Don Maynard took a measure of consolation, despite his team's 7-7 second-place division finish behind Miami. Maynard caught pass number 632 to eclipse Baltimore great Raymond Berry as the NFL's all-time reception leader.

If creature comfort could soothe the sting of second place, fans in Kansas City didn't have it so bad. The Chiefs (8-6) were runners-up to Oakland (10-3-1) for the AFL's Western Division title, but their new Arrowhead Stadium had room for 78,067 spectators, 50,000 of whom sat between the end lines. Arrowhead became the new prototype for non-domed, football-only stadiums.

At the beginning of the year, when the rules makers moved the hashmarks, or "inbound lines," three yards toward the middle of the field from either sideline, their aim was to open up the passing game by blunting the

Powerhouse Miami Dolphins running back Larry Csonka.

effect of the increasingly popular zone defense. The move may have had a residual, or even direct, effect on the running game's success, as a record 10 backs ran for at least 1,000 yards. The winner of this derby was Buffalo's O.J. Simpson with 1,251 yards. The list extended to Miami's Eugene (Mercury) Morris, who, the league noticed, had been erroneously charged with a nine-yard loss that should have been marked as a fumble by quarterback Earl Morrall. Morris finished with an even 1,000 yards and joined Larry Csonka (1,117 yards) as the first teammates to gain 1,000 yards each in the same season. Atlanta running back Dave Hampton made it to 1,001, but carried the ball once too often, losing 6 yards on his final carry and dropping to 995.

1972

AMERICAN CONFERENCE

EASTERN DIVISION	W	L	T	Pct.	Pts.	OP
Miami	14	0	0	1.000	385	171
N.Y. Jets	7	7	0	.500	367	324
Baltimore	5	9	0	.357	235	252
Buffalo	4	9	1	.321	257	377
New England	3	11	0	.214	192	446
CENTRAL DIVISION	**W**	**L**	**T**	**Pct.**	**Pts.**	**OP**
Pittsburgh	11	3	0	.786	343	175
Cleveland*	10	4	0	.714	268	249
Cincinnati	8	6	0	.571	299	229
Houston	1	13	0	.071	164	380
WESTERN DIVISION	**W**	**L**	**T**	**Pct.**	**Pts.**	**OP**
Oakland	10	3	1	.750	365	248
Kansas City	8	6	0	.571	287	254
Denver	5	9	0	.357	325	350
San Diego	4	9	1	.321	264	344

NATIONAL CONFERENCE

EASTERN DIVISION	W	L	T	Pct.	Pts.	OP
Washington	11	3	0	.786	336	218
Dallas*	10	4	0	.714	319	240
N.Y. Giants	8	6	0	.571	331	247
St. Louis	4	9	1	.321	193	303
Philadelphia	2	11	1	.179	145	352
CENTRAL DIVISION	**W**	**L**	**T**	**Pct.**	**Pts.**	**OP**
Green Bay	10	4	0	.714	304	226
Detroit	8	5	1	.607	339	290
Minnesota	7	7	0	.500	301	252
Chicago	4	9	1	.321	225	275
WESTERN DIVISION	**W**	**L**	**T**	**Pct.**	**Pts.**	**OP**
San Francisco	8	5	1	.607	353	249
Atlanta	7	7	0	.500	269	274
Los Angeles	6	7	1	.464	291	286
New Orleans	2	11	1	.179	215	361

**Wild Card qualifier for playoffs*

Divisional playoffs: PITTSBURGH 13, Oakland 7; MIAMI 20, Cleveland 14
AFC championship: Miami 21, PITTSBURGH 17
Divisional playoffs: Dallas 30, SAN FRANCISCO 28; WASHINGTON 16, Green Bay 3
NFC championship: WASHINGTON 26, Dallas 3
Super Bowl VII: Miami (AFC) 14, Washington (NFC) 7, at Memorial Coliseum, Los Angeles, Calif.

1973

No sooner had the 1,000-yard plateau been mocked by a slew of running backs than their leader went ahead and doubled the standard. Having set a single-game record with 250 yards against New England on opening day, Buffalo's O.J. Simpson finished the year with a total of 2,003, rushing for 200 yards against the New York Jets in a snowstorm at Shea Stadium. (He entered

O.J. Simpson broke the NFL single-season rushing record.

Miami coach Don Shula and quarterback Bob Griese followed up their perfect 1972 season with a second consecutive NFL title.

needing 61 yards to pass Jim Brown's one-season record of 1,863.)

Give credit to Simpson's offensive line, the vaunted Electric Company (O.J. had become "Juice," hence the need for a power source): center Mike Montler, guards Joe DeLamielleure and Reggie McKenzie, tackles Steve Foley and Donnie Green, and tight end Paul Seymour.

But 1,000 yards was linked to another name in 1973, as Green Bay's John Brockington became the first man in NFL history to reach that total in each of his first three seasons.

Congress passed a bill that lifted the hometown blackout on any game sold out 72 hours before kickoff. The new law prompted the addition of "no-shows" to the NFL glossary, to describe those who bought tickets but chose television on game day.

The up-and-down Cincinnati Bengals won the AFC

Central with a 10-4 record, edging Pittsburgh, also 10-4, on the basis of a better record in intraconference games. Quarterback Ken Anderson, wide receiver Isaac Curtis, and running backs Essex Johnson and Boobie Clark were the offensive leaders for the Bengals, who lost 34-16 to Miami in a divisional playoff game. The Dolphins rumbled to their second straight Super Bowl victory, 24-7 over Minnesota. Miami fullback Larry Csonka set a Super Bowl record, rushing for 145 yards at Rice Stadium in Houston. The Dolphins' "No-Name" (read "No Stars, Just A Well-Coordinated Unit Under Assistant Bill Arnsparger") defense unscrambled quarterback Fran Tarkenton.

As the NFL appointed a committee, headed by Pittsburgh Steelers president Dan Rooney, to explore the possibilities of future expansion, others outside the league were starting from scratch. An October meeting in Los Angeles ended with the announcement that the World Football League would begin play in 1974.

1973

AMERICAN CONFERENCE

EASTERN DIVISION

	W	L	T	Pct.	Pts.	OP
Miami	12	2	0	.857	343	150
Buffalo	9	5	0	.643	259	230
New England	5	9	0	.357	258	300
Baltimore	4	10	0	.286	226	341
N.Y. Jets	4	10	0	.286	240	306

CENTRAL DIVISION

	W	L	T	Pct.	Pts.	OP
Cincinnati	10	4	0	.714	286	231
Pittsburgh*	10	4	0	.714	347	210
Cleveland	7	5	2	.571	234	255
Houston	1	13	0	.071	199	447

WESTERN DIVISION

	W	L	T	Pct.	Pts.	OP
Oakland	9	4	1	.679	292	175
Denver	7	5	2	.571	354	296
Kansas City	7	5	2	.571	231	192
San Diego	2	11	1	.179	188	386

NATIONAL CONFERENCE

EASTERN DIVISION

	W	L	T	Pct.	Pts.	OP
Dallas	10	4	0	.714	382	203
Washington*	10	4	0	.714	325	198
Philadelphia	5	8	1	.393	310	393
St. Louis	4	9	1	.321	286	365
N.Y. Giants	2	11	1	.179	226	362

CENTRAL DIVISION

	W	L	T	Pct.	Pts.	OP
Minnesota	12	2	0	.857	296	168
Detroit	6	7	1	.464	271	247
Green Bay	5	7	2	.429	202	259
Chicago	3	11	0	.214	195	334

WESTERN DIVISION

	W	L	T	Pct.	Pts.	OP
Los Angeles	12	2	0	.857	388	178
Atlanta	9	5	0	.643	318	224
New Orleans	5	9	0	.357	163	312
San Francisco	5	9	0	.357	262	319

**Wild Card qualifier for playoffs*

Cincinnati won division title on the basis of a better conference record than Pittsburgh (8-3 to 7-4). Dallas won division title on the basis of a better point differential vs. Washington (net 13 points).

Divisional playoffs: OAKLAND 33, Pittsburgh 14; MIAMI 34, Cincinnati 16
AFC championship: MIAMI 27, Oakland 10
Divisional playoffs: MINNESOTA 27, Washington 20; DALLAS 27, Los Angeles 16
NFC championship: Minnesota 27, DALLAS 10
Super Bowl VIII: Miami (AFC) 24, Minnesota (NFC) 7, at Rice Stadium, Houston, Tex.

1974

When the season opened, new rules took effect: Defensive players were allowed only one ''bump'' or ''chuck,'' a reaction to the evolving ''bump-and-run'' style of pass coverage. On punts, only two outside men from the kicking team were allowed downfield before the ball was kicked. The penalty for offensive holding was reduced to 10 yards. Receivers no longer could make ''crack-back'' blocks below the waist.

Goal posts were moved to the end lines. Teams kicked off from the 35-yard line instead of the 40. Miss a field goal from outside the 20, and your opponent got to start from the original line of scrimmage.

The results were predictable: more touchdowns, fewer field goals. The revised punting rules led to fewer fair catches and longer runbacks.

But even before the season began, owners and players had found themselves deadlocked over a new collective-bargaining agreement. The old four-year contract had expired, and it wasn't until August 28 that an interim agreement could be reached.

Cincinnati quarterback Ken Anderson and Baltimore quarterback Bert Jones played a game of ''Can You Top This?'' Anderson completed 16 consecutive passes against the Colts, an NFL record. Jones must have studied Anderson well, because a month later, he broke the record with 17 in a row against the New York Jets.

St. Louis, under coach Don Coryell, was in the playoffs for the first time since the club had moved down from Chicago. The highlight of the postseason tournament, however, was Oakland's last-minute 28-26 victory over Miami in the first round of the AFC divisional playoffs.

The Raiders' magic vanished a week later when Pittsburgh won the AFC championship 24-13 in Oakland. The Steelers made their first Super Bowl trip a successful one, giving owner Art Rooney his first championship in 42 years.

Tackle Joe Greene (75) and end L.C. Greenwood provided much of the steel in Pittsburgh's impenetrable Steel Curtain defense.

A 16-6 victory over three-time Super Bowl loser Minnesota at Tulane Stadium in New Orleans included a record 158-yard rushing performance by Franco Harris and the defensive dominance of a line nicknamed the Steel Curtain—ends Dwight White and L.C. Greenwood and tackles Joe Greene and Ernie Holmes.

Lydell Mitchell of the Baltimore Colts set a record for running backs, and led all NFL receivers, with 72 catches in 1974.

1974

AMERICAN CONFERENCE

EASTERN DIVISION

	W	L	T	Pct.	Pts.	OP
Miami	11	3	0	.786	327	216
Buffalo*	9	5	0	.643	264	244
New England	7	7	0	.500	348	289
N.Y. Jets	7	7	0	.500	279	300
Baltimore	2	12	0	.143	190	329

CENTRAL DIVISION

	W	L	T	Pct.	Pts.	OP
Pittsburgh	10	3	1	.750	305	189
Cincinnati	7	7	0	.500	283	259
Houston	7	7	0	.500	236	282
Cleveland	4	10	0	.286	251	344

WESTERN DIVISION

	W	L	T	Pct.	Pts.	OP
Oakland	12	2	0	.857	355	228
Denver	7	6	1	.536	302	294
Kansas City	5	9	0	.357	233	293
San Diego	5	9	0	.357	212	285

NATIONAL CONFERENCE

EASTERN DIVISION

	W	L	T	Pct.	Pts.	OP
St. Louis	10	4	0	.714	285	218
Washington*	10	4	0	.714	320	196
Dallas	8	6	0	.571	297	235
Philadelphia	7	7	0	.500	242	217
N.Y. Giants	2	12	0	.143	195	299

CENTRAL DIVISION

	W	L	T	Pct.	Pts.	OP
Minnesota	10	4	0	.714	310	195
Detroit	7	7	0	.500	256	270
Green Bay	6	8	0	.429	210	206
Chicago	4	10	0	.286	152	279

WESTERN DIVISION

	W	L	T	Pct.	Pts.	OP
Los Angeles	10	4	0	.714	263	181
San Francisco	6	8	0	.429	226	236
New Orleans	5	9	0	.357	166	263
Atlanta	3	11	0	.214	111	271

**Wild Card qualifier for playoffs*

St. Louis won division title because of a two-game sweep over Washington.

Divisional playoffs: OAKLAND 28, Miami 26; PITTSBURGH 32, Buffalo 14

AFC championship: Pittsburgh 24, OAKLAND 13

Divisional playoffs: MINNESOTA 30, St. Louis 14; LOS ANGELES 19, Washington 10

NFC championship: MINNESOTA 14, Los Angeles 10

Super Bowl IX: Pittsburgh (AFC) 16, Minnesota (NFC) 6, at Tulane Stadium, New Orleans, La.

1975

"The Packers have a long road back to the top," said Bart Starr, taking over as head coach of the team he had quarterbacked to five NFL titles. It was a remark anyone could have made, witness Green Bay's 45-49-5 record since its last title under Vince Lombardi in 1967.

Starr would go 4-10 in 1975 and 53-77-3 in a nine-year period before being replaced in 1983.

The league abolished the "taxi squad," a kind of designated reserve tank that had picked up its name when former Cleveland owner Mickey McBride, who also had a taxi company, employed his leftover players as cabbies during the 1940s, the better to keep them on hand in case roster players were injured.

The Detroit Lions became the first NFL team to play its home games under a Teflon roof, moving into the Pontiac Silverdome (capacity: 80,638). Meanwhile, the New Orleans Saints relocated to the Louisiana Superdome (capacity: 71,647), with its 273-foot ceiling and five giant television screens, all mounted on a single carousel that hung above midfield.

One quarterback, Minnesota's Fran Tarkenton, had a banner year, while another, Oakland's George Blanda, bade a hero's farewell. Tarkenton set all-time records for career touchdown passes (291), completions (2,931), and attempts (5,225), all formerly held by Johnny Unitas, who had retired in 1974. Blanda left the game at age 49, with records for most active seasons (26), games played (340), consecutive games played (224), points scored (2,002), field goals (335), and points after touchdown (959).

The Raiders went 11-3 to win the AFC West, but finished their season on the Pittsburgh Steelers' 15-yard line at icy Three Rivers Stadium. Linebacker Jack Lambert recovered three fumbles in the Steelers' 16-10 victory for the AFC championship.

For the Houston Oilers, 10-4 under new head coach Oail ("Cain't nobody spell it or pronounce it or any-

Acrobatic Pittsburgh wide receiver Lynn Swann was named the most valuable player in the Steelers' Super Bowl X victory.

thing'') A. Phillips, affectionately nicknamed ''Bum,'' this was the first winning season since 1967. Credit Phillips's switch to a three-man defensive front and Dan Pastorini's quarterbacking for the upturn.

You could get technical about it and remind everyone that the Kansas City Chiefs had advanced from a second-place finish to a Super Bowl victory in 1969, but theirs was *de facto* wild-card status. This time around, the Dallas Cowboys became the first wild-card team to reach the NFL's ultimate game since that designation became official. It was academic. The Cowboys fell to dynasty-bound Pittsburgh in Miami's Orange Bowl, 21-17.

The World Football League went out of business in October.

1975

AMERICAN CONFERENCE

EASTERN DIVISION	W	L	T	Pct.	Pts.	OP
Baltimore	10	4	0	.714	395	269
Miami	10	4	0	.714	357	222
Buffalo	8	6	0	.571	420	355
New England	3	11	0	.214	258	358
N.Y. Jets	3	11	0	.214	258	433
CENTRAL DIVISION	**W**	**L**	**T**	**Pct.**	**Pts.**	**OP**
Pittsburgh	12	2	0	.857	373	162
Cincinnati*	11	3	0	.786	340	246
Houston	10	4	0	.714	293	226
Cleveland	3	11	0	.214	218	372
WESTERN DIVISION	**W**	**L**	**T**	**Pct.**	**Pts.**	**OP**
Oakland	11	3	0	.786	375	255
Denver	6	8	0	.429	254	307
Kansas City	5	9	0	.357	282	341
San Diego	2	12	0	.143	189	345

NATIONAL CONFERENCE

EASTERN DIVISION	W	L	T	Pct.	Pts.	OP
St. Louis	11	3	0	.786	356	276
Dallas*	10	4	0	.714	350	268
Washington	8	6	0	.571	325	276
N.Y. Giants	5	9	0	.357	216	306
Philadelphia	4	10	0	.286	225	302
CENTRAL DIVISION	**W**	**L**	**T**	**Pct.**	**Pts.**	**OP**
Minnesota	12	2	0	.857	377	180
Detroit	7	7	0	.500	245	262
Chicago	4	10	0	.286	191	379
Green Bay	4	10	0	.286	226	285
WESTERN DIVISION	**W**	**L**	**T**	**Pct.**	**Pts.**	**OP**
Los Angeles	12	2	0	.857	312	135
San Francisco	5	9	0	.357	255	286
Atlanta	4	10	0	.286	240	289
New Orleans	2	12	0	.143	165	360

**Wild Card qualifier for playoffs*

Baltimore won division title on the basis of a two-game sweep over Miami.

Divisional playoffs: PITTSBURGH 28, Baltimore 10; OAKLAND 31, Cincinnati 28

AFC championship: PITTSBURGH 16, Oakland 10

Divisional playoffs: LOS ANGELES 35, St. Louis 23; Dallas 17, MINNESOTA 14

NFC championship: Dallas 37, LOS ANGELES 7

Super Bowl X: Pittsburgh (AFC) 21, Dallas (NFC) 17, at Orange Bowl, Miami, Fla.

1976

Seattle and Tampa Bay housed their new teams, the Seahawks and Buccaneers, in the Kingdome and Tampa Stadium. The latter was expanded to seat 71,400, while the former boasted the world's largest free-standing roof.

The NFL draft was delayed until the second week of April, and the Buccaneers made Oklahoma's Lee Roy Selmon, a defensive lineman, their first pick. They got to go first by winning a coin flip, which turned out to be their only victory of the year. On the field, they went 0-14. The Seahawks fared better at 2-12, building their offense around the passing combination of an undrafted free agent, Jim Zorn, who set a record for passing yardage by a rookie (2,571), and rookie wide receiver Steve Largent, who caught 54 passes to rank third in the NFC. The Buccaneers spent their first year in the AFC, then permanently swapped conferences with the Seahawks.

The rest of the NFL went about revising the record book some more. The 10-man 1,000-yard extravaganza of 1972 was surpassed when O.J. Simpson led 12 backs beyond the mark. Part of Simpson's 1,503-yard total was a single-game-record 273-yard performance against Detroit on Thanksgiving Day.

Other milestones included Fran Tarkenton's finishing the season with 41,801 yards passing, an all-time record that moved Johnny Unitas into second place. Tarkenton's Minnesota teammate Jim Marshall, of wrong-way fame, moved past George Blanda to lead the all-time consecutive games list at 236. Oakland's Ken Stabler completed passes at a 66.7 percentage, the NFL's best since Sammy Baugh of Washington connected on 70.3 in 1945.

In an AFC Divisional Playoff Game against New England, a controversial roughing-the-passer call set up Stabler's scrambling, diving touchdown run, and the Raiders advanced to the AFC Championship Game. There, they met a Pittsburgh team that had lost running backs

The Oakland Raiders never could be counted out of any game with resourceful Kenny (The Snake) Stabler at quarterback.

Franco Harris and Rocky Bleier to injuries, and the Steelers' dynasty went on hold, 24-7. Conversely, the AFC title gave the Raiders their first trip to the Super Bowl in 10 years, after having lost six AFC Championship Games in the interim.

One Super Bowl tradition lived on. Minnesota lost its fourth Super Bowl in as many attempts. In game XI at Pasadena's Rose Bowl, Stabler and wide receiver Fred Biletnikoff shredded the Vikings' secondary, and running back Clarence Davis rushed for 137 yards, part of the Raiders' record 429 yards of total offense en route to a 32-14 victory.

1976

AMERICAN CONFERENCE

EASTERN DIVISION

	W	L	T	Pct.	Pts.	OP
Baltimore	11	3	0	.786	417	246
New England*	11	3	0	.786	376	236
Miami	6	8	0	.429	263	264
N.Y. Jets	3	11	0	.214	169	383
Buffalo	2	12	0	.143	245	363

CENTRAL DIVISION

	W	L	T	Pct.	Pts.	OP
Pittsburgh	10	4	0	.714	342	138
Cincinnati	10	4	0	.714	335	210
Cleveland	9	5	0	.643	267	287
Houston	5	9	0	.357	222	273

WESTERN DIVISION

	W	L	T	Pct.	Pts.	OP
Oakland	13	1	0	.929	350	237
Denver	9	5	0	.643	315	206
San Diego	6	8	0	.429	248	285
Kansas City	5	9	0	.357	290	376
Tampa Bay	0	14	0	.000	125	412

NATIONAL CONFERENCE

EASTERN DIVISION

	W	L	T	Pct.	Pts.	OP
Dallas	11	3	0	.786	296	194
Washington*	10	4	0	.714	291	217
St. Louis	10	4	0	.714	309	267
Philadelphia	4	10	0	.286	165	286
N.Y. Giants	3	11	0	.214	170	250

CENTRAL DIVISION

	W	L	T	Pct.	Pts.	OP
Minnesota	11	2	1	.821	305	176
Chicago	7	7	0	.500	253	216
Detroit	6	8	0	.429	262	220
Green Bay	5	9	0	.357	218	299

WESTERN DIVISION

	W	L	T	Pct.	Pts.	OP
Los Angeles	10	3	1	.750	351	190
San Francisco	8	6	0	.571	270	190
Atlanta	4	10	0	.286	172	312
New Orleans	4	10	0	.286	253	346
Seattle	2	12	0	.143	229	429

**Wild Card qualifier for playoffs*

Baltimore won division title on the basis of a better division record than New England (7-1 to 6-2). Pittsburgh won division title because of a two-game sweep over Cincinnati. Washington won Wild Card berth over St. Louis because of a two-game sweep over Cardinals.

Divisional playoffs: OAKLAND 24, New England 21; Pittsburgh 40, BALTIMORE 14

AFC championship: OAKLAND 24, Pittsburgh 7

Divisional playoffs: MINNESOTA 35, Washington 20; Los Angeles 14, DALLAS 12

NFC championship: MINNESOTA 24, Los Angeles 13

Super Bowl XI: Oakland (AFC) 32, Minnesota (NFC) 14, at Rose Bowl, Pasadena, Calif.

1977

The spoils of Tampa Bay's winless maiden season, such as they were, began (and probably ended) with the first pick in the draft, and the Buccaneers drew mild surprise around the league by taking USC running back Ricky Bell. Mild, because in bypassing Heisman Trophy winner Tony Dorsett of Pittsburgh, Buccaneers coach John McKay was opting for a man he'd known two years earlier while coaching him with the Trojans.

Seattle, meanwhile, had traded its first pick to Dallas, which grabbed Dorsett. Winning the Heisman and being the focal point of the first round, it turned out, were only two-thirds of a pre-NFL triple play for the little speedster, who announced that from then on, when his last name was pronounced, the emphasis would be placed on the second syllable, not the first.

The trend toward a higher-scoring, safer game continued, as rules changes emphasized more freedom for the passing attack and protection from two techniques—the head slap by defensive linemen and clipping by wide receivers, even in the "legal clipping zone." Pass defenders were limited to only one contact with a receiver, bringing bump-and-run coverage a step closer to its knees.

From safety to serenity: The National Football League Players Association and the NFL Management Council ratified a collective bargaining agreement that would extend until mid-1982. Highlights of the agreement: Contributions to the pension plan for the next five years—plus the years 1974, 1975, and 1976—would come to more than $55 million. A player would be vested in the pension plan after four years, down from the previous five. The player limit was set at 43 per club. Minimum salaries were increased, as were paychecks for preseason and postseason play.

Never mind the rules changes designed to open up the passing game, seemed to be the message of running backs O.J. Simpson and Walter Payton. The latter

Denver's swarming Orange Crush defense buried ball carriers.

erased the former's single-game rushing record when he went 275 yards against Minnesota on his way to a league-leading 1,852-yard season, third-highest in NFL history. For his part, Simpson, despite a knee injury, became only the second back to gain 10,000 yards in his career, joining Jim Brown.

Minnesota kicker Fred Cox reached a similar height, passing Lou Groza to take over second place behind George Blanda on the all-time scoring list. Cox's Vikings won the NFC Central, and, in the first round of the playoffs, improvised in the muddy bottom of the Los Angeles Coliseum. With a December rainstorm inundating southern California, the Vikings—with Bob Lee substituting at quarterback for injured Fran Tarkenton—took advantage of what footing there was in the first quarter and took a 7-0 lead over the Rams. The two teams spun their wheels in the slop for the next 45 minutes, and Minnesota won the Mud Bowl 14-7.

Dallas, having easily dispensed with wild-card Chicago, easily dispensed with the Vikings the following week, then went on to easily dispense with Denver in Super Bowl XII, 27-10. The Broncos had arrived at the Superdome in New Orleans on the strength of a defense nicknamed the Orange Crush, led by linebacker Randy Gradishar and defensive end Lyle Alzado. However, the day belonged to Dallas's Flex defense, well-publicized for its complexity and befitting the team that had pioneered and perfected the use of computerized scouting. Defenders Harvey Martin (end) and Randy White (tackle) represented the unit as they picked up the Super Bowl's first (and still its only) co-most valuable player award.

The Broncos and first-year head coach Robert (Red) Miller had become a regional phenomenon. When the Oakland Raiders came to town, the fans dressed for "Orange Sunday" at Mile High Stadium, where no-shows dare not show their faces after their first offense. The Broncos had entered a new age of competence, just by reaching New Orleans. Their route was littered with conference giants such as Pittsburgh and Oakland, the latter "fresh" from a dramatic double-sudden-death overtime victory over the Baltimore Colts.

No account of the 1977 season, however brief, should end without filling in the fate of Tampa Bay. After extending their 0-14 of 1976 to 0-26, the longest losing streak in NFL history, the Buccaneers met New Orleans at the Superdome on December 11. Scoring three touchdowns on interceptions, they earned the first victory in the history of the franchise, 33-14. After returning to an airport crowd of 8,000, the Buccaneers proved they could win at home, finishing the season with a 17-7 victory over St. Louis.

1977

AMERICAN CONFERENCE

EASTERN DIVISION

	W	L	T	Pct.	Pts.	OP
Baltimore	10	4	0	.714	295	221
Miami	10	4	0	.714	313	197
New England	9	5	0	.643	278	217
N.Y. Jets	3	11	0	.214	191	300
Buffalo	3	11	0	.214	160	313

CENTRAL DIVISION

	W	L	T	Pct.	Pts.	OP
Pittsburgh	9	5	0	.643	283	243
Houston	8	6	0	.571	299	230
Cincinnati	8	6	0	.571	238	235
Cleveland	6	8	0	.429	269	267

WESTERN DIVISION

	W	L	T	Pct.	Pts.	OP
Denver	12	2	0	.857	274	148
Oakland*	11	3	0	.786	351	230
San Diego	7	7	0	.500	222	205
Seattle	5	9	0	.357	282	373
Kansas City	2	12	0	.143	225	349

NATIONAL CONFERENCE

EASTERN DIVISION

	W	L	T	Pct.	Pts.	OP
Dallas	12	2	0	.857	345	212
Washington	9	5	0	.643	196	189
St. Louis	7	7	0	.500	272	287
Philadelphia	5	9	0	.357	220	207
N.Y. Giants	5	9	0	.357	181	265

CENTRAL DIVISION

	W	L	T	Pct.	Pts.	OP
Minnesota	9	5	0	.643	231	227
Chicago*	9	5	0	.643	255	253
Detroit	6	8	0	.429	183	252
Green Bay	4	10	0	.286	134	219
Tampa Bay	2	12	0	.143	103	223

WESTERN DIVISION

	W	L	T	Pct.	Pts.	OP
Los Angeles	10	4	0	.714	302	146
Atlanta	7	7	0	.500	179	129
San Francisco	5	9	0	.357	220	260
New Orleans	3	11	0	.214	232	336

**Wild Card qualifier for playoffs*

Baltimore won division title on the basis of a better conference record than Miami (9-3 to 8-4). Chicago won a Wild Card berth over Washington on the basis of best net points in conference games (plus 48 net points to plus 4).

Divisional playoffs: DENVER 34, Pittsburgh 21; Oakland 37, BALTIMORE 31, sudden death overtime

AFC championship: DENVER 20, Oakland 17

Divisional playoffs: DALLAS 37, Chicago 7; Minnesota 14, LOS ANGELES 7

NFC championship: DALLAS 23, Minnesota 6

Super Bowl XII: Dallas (NFC) 27, Denver (AFC) 10, at Louisiana Superdome, New Orleans, La.

1978

More bad news for pass defenders: A "bump" zone inhibited them from making contact with receivers beyond a point five yards from the line of scrimmage. For offenses, the green light got greener.

The league added a seventh official, the side judge, to keep an eye on new technicalities in the vicinity of scrimmage, such as the new bump rule and liberalized pass-blocking that allowed an offensive lineman to extend his arms. The number of regular-season games was increased from 14 to 16, while preseason games were cut from 6 to 4. A new television contract was worth over $5 million to each club. Another wild-card team was added to the playoff structure, setting up an extra weekend for games between the two wild-card teams in each conference.

The Tampa Bay defense, featuring the Selmon brothers, linebacker Dewey (61) and end Lee Roy (63), came of age early.

Another familiar sight was the revolving door, as nine teams changed head coaches before the season began—one of them twice. The new men: Jack Pardee in Washington, Neill Armstrong in Chicago replacing Pardee, Bud Wilkinson in St. Louis, Sam Rutigliano in Cleveland, Marv Levy in Kansas City, Dick Nolan in New Orleans, Monte Clark in Detroit, Chuck Knox in Buffalo, and George Allen from Washington to replace Knox in Los Angeles. Allen was fired even before the season began, and Ray Malavasi was named to the position.

Four more teams had new coaches before the end of the season. After four games, Tommy Prothro resigned in San Diego and was replaced by Don Coryell. The next week, Cincinnati replaced Bill Johnson with Homer Rice. A 1-8 record in San Francisco preceded the firing of Pete McCulley, who was followed by Fred O'Connor. And before the season finale, New England's Chuck Fairbanks announced he was resigning to become head coach at Colorado. Although the legal complications continued for several months, Fairbanks was succeeded in the last game by assistants Ron Erhardt and Hank Bullough.

Minnesota's Fran Tarkenton and Rickey Young revised a few passing and receiving categories of the NFL record book. Tarkenton increased his own marks for number of completions and attempts, going 345 for 572. Young set a record for receptions by a running back, and also led the league with his 88 catches.

Houston had used the first pick in the 1978 draft to take Heisman Trophy-winning halfback Earl Campbell of Texas, and the early dividends included Campbell's leading the Oilers to the AFC Championship Game with the best-ever rookie season for a ball carrier, 1,450 yards.

Oilers quarterback Dan Pastorini, when asked what it felt like to hand off to Campbell, replied, "Comfortable." The feeling must have been in full force on November 20, as Campbell rushed for 199 yards and four

Hard-running Earl Campbell was the league's top draft choice.

touchdowns in a seesaw 35-30 victory over Miami. Comfort had its limits, however, as Pastorini suffered rib injuries during the course of the season and had to be fitted with a special device for the playoffs. Wearing the flak jacket of inventor Byron Donzis (whose quality-control tests included swinging a baseball bat into the rib cage of his guinea pig—often Donzis himself), Pastorini completed 20 of 29 passing attempts in a 17-9 AFC wild-card game victory over Miami. The following week, again protected by the vest, he bombed the New England Patriots (12 of 20 for 200 yards and three touchdowns) in a 31-14 victory.

The Oilers were thrashed 34-5 by Pittsburgh in the AFC Championship Game, and that set up the first rematch in Super Bowl history, the Steelers versus the Dallas Cowboys. The Cowboys, in the opening two rounds, beat Atlanta, a wild-card winner over Philadelphia, then went on to shut out Los Angeles. Their rendezvous with the Steelers at Miami's Orange Bowl was enough to engage thousands in "best Super Bowl of all" debates (X versus XIII) well into the next decade, and maybe another. Not surprisingly, it was Pittsburgh, behind quarterback Terry Bradshaw's record four touchdown passes, which held on for an exciting 35-31 victory in the highest-scoring game in Super Bowl history.

1978

AMERICAN CONFERENCE

EASTERN DIVISION

	W	L	T	Pct.	Pts.	OP
New England	11	5	0	.688	358	286
Miami*	11	5	0	.688	372	254
N.Y. Jets	8	8	0	.500	359	364
Buffalo	5	11	0	.313	302	354
Baltimore	5	11	0	.313	239	421

CENTRAL DIVISION

	W	L	T	Pct.	Pts.	OP
Pittsburgh	14	2	0	.875	356	195
Houston*	10	6	0	.625	283	298
Cleveland	8	8	0	.500	334	356
Cincinnati	4	12	0	.250	252	284

WESTERN DIVISION

	W	L	T	Pct.	Pts.	OP
Denver	10	6	0	.625	282	198
Oakland	9	7	0	.563	311	283
Seattle	9	7	0	.563	345	358
San Diego	9	7	0	.563	355	309
Kansas City	4	12	0	.250	243	327

NATIONAL CONFERENCE

EASTERN DIVISION

	W	L	T	Pct.	Pts.	OP
Dallas	12	4	0	.750	384	208
Philadelphia*	9	7	0	.563	270	250
Washington	8	8	0	.500	273	283
St. Louis	6	10	0	.375	248	296
N.Y. Giants	6	10	0	.375	264	298

CENTRAL DIVISION

	W	L	T	Pct.	Pts.	OP
Minnesota	8	7	1	.531	294	306
Green Bay	8	7	1	.531	249	269
Detroit	7	9	0	.438	290	300
Chicago	7	9	0	.438	253	274
Tampa Bay	5	11	0	.313	241	259

WESTERN DIVISION

	W	L	T	Pct.	Pts.	OP
Los Angeles	12	4	0	.750	316	245
Atlanta*	9	7	0	.563	240	290
New Orleans	7	9	0	.438	281	298
San Francisco	2	14	0	.125	219	350

**Wild Card qualifier for playoffs*

New England won division title on the basis of a better division record than Miami (6-2 to 5-3). Minnesota won division title because of a better head-to-head record against Green Bay (1-0-1).

First round playoff: Houston 17, MIAMI 9

Divisional playoffs: Houston 31, NEW ENGLAND 14; PITTSBURGH 33, Denver 10

AFC championship: PITTSBURGH 34, Houston 5

First round playoff: ATLANTA 14, Philadelphia 13

Divisional playoffs: DALLAS 27, Atlanta 20; LOS ANGELES 34, Minnesota 10

NFC championship: Dallas 28, LOS ANGELES 0

Super Bowl XIII: Pittsburgh (AFC) 35, Dallas (NFC) 31, at Orange Bowl, Miami, Fla.

1979

Air raid! As an appropriate commemorative of the NFL's sixtieth year, San Diego's Dan Fouts broke Joe Namath's single-season passing yardage record with 4,082 yards. It was the infancy of "Air Coryell," named for head coach Don Coryell, a proponent of Sid Gillman's upfield, or "vertical," passing attitude. Among Fouts's

San Diego quarterback Dan Fouts was the pilot of "Air Coryell."

receivers was rookie tight end Kellen Winslow, essentially a wide receiver in San Diego's system before breaking his leg. The Chargers, not incidentally, were on their way to the championship of the AFC West.

If Fouts was telling his people to "go long," San Francisco's Steve DeBerg had people going everywhere. New 49ers coach Bill Walsh, up from a successful term at Stanford, installed a multiple-choice passing scheme that took full advantage of running backs as receivers. DeBerg's 347 completions in 1979 established a single-season record.

Philadelphia wide receiver Harold Carmichael set an NFL record for consecutive games with at least one reception, 112.

The retirement of Fran Tarkenton, after 16 years at quarterback for Minnesota and the New York Giants, froze the major career passing records for a while. Tarkenton left the game with lifetime marks for attempts (6,467), completions (3,686), yards (47,003), and touchdown passes (342).

Player safety was the guidepost for rules changes, which prohibited blocking below the waist on kickoffs, punts, and field-goal attempts. The no-crackback zone was extended. Torn or altered equipment was prohibited, as were exposed pads—all hazards. And chalk up another for the passing game: Officials were instructed to whistle a play dead if the quarterback clearly was in the grasp of a defender. (Interpretation of this tricky concept would give officials, players, coaches, announcers, fans—everybody—their moments in the coming years. "Was he in the grasp or wasn't he? You make the call.")

The Los Angeles Rams, in their final season at the Los Angeles Memorial Coliseum before moving 32 miles south to Anaheim Stadium, won their seventh consecutive NFC West title despite a number of key injuries. Two minutes remained in a divisional playoff game when Vince Ferragamo hit Billy Waddy with a touchdown pass for a 21-19 victory over Dallas. By the

The dynastic Steelers, with quarterback Terry Bradshaw and center Mike Webster, won an unprecedented fourth Super Bowl.

time the Rams had defeated Tampa Bay 9-0 for the NFC championship (the Buccaneers had shed their doormat status, going 10-6 to win the NFC Central title), the Pittsburgh Steelers had rolled through the AFC, handily defeating Miami 31-14 and Houston 27-13. The Steelers were in the Super Bowl for the fourth time.

Playing before 103,985 at the Rose Bowl in Pasadena and a record television audience of 35,330,000 homes, Pittsburgh won its fourth Lombardi Trophy, overcoming the Rams' third-quarter 19-17 lead. The go-ahead touchdown was a 73-yard pass from Terry Bradshaw to wide receiver John Stallworth. The Steelers added a grace touchdown for a final count of 31-19. Bradshaw won his second automobile as the recipient of the game's most valuable player award.

1979

AMERICAN CONFERENCE

EASTERN DIVISION

	W	L	T	Pct.	Pts.	OP
Miami	10	6	0	.625	341	257
New England	9	7	0	.563	411	326
N.Y. Jets	8	8	0	.500	337	383
Buffalo	7	9	0	.438	268	279
Baltimore	5	11	0	.313	271	351

CENTRAL DIVISION

	W	L	T	Pct.	Pts.	OP
Pittsburgh	12	4	0	.750	416	262
Houston*	11	5	0	.688	362	331
Cleveland	9	7	0	.563	359	352
Cincinnati	4	12	0	.250	337	421

WESTERN DIVISION

	W	L	T	Pct.	Pts.	OP
San Diego	12	4	0	.750	411	246
Denver*	10	6	0	.625	289	262
Seattle	9	7	0	.563	378	372
Oakland	9	7	0	.563	365	337
Kansas City	7	9	0	.438	238	262

NATIONAL CONFERENCE

EASTERN DIVISION

	W	L	T	Pct.	Pts.	OP
Dallas	11	5	0	.688	371	313
Philadelphia*	11	5	0	.688	339	282
Washington	10	6	0	.625	348	295
N.Y. Giants	6	10	0	.375	237	323
St. Louis	5	11	0	.313	307	358

CENTRAL DIVISION

	W	L	T	Pct.	Pts.	OP
Tampa Bay	10	6	0	.625	273	237
Chicago*	10	6	0	.625	306	249
Minnesota	7	9	0	.438	259	337
Green Bay	5	11	0	.313	246	316
Detroit	2	14	0	.125	219	365

WESTERN DIVISION

	W	L	T	Pct.	Pts.	OP
Los Angeles	9	7	0	.563	323	309
New Orleans	8	8	0	.500	370	360
Atlanta	6	10	0	.375	300	388
San Francisco	2	14	0	.125	308	416

**Wild Card qualifier for playoffs*

Dallas won division title because of a better conference record than Philadelphia (10-2 to 9-3). Tampa Bay won division title because of a better division record than Chicago (6-2 to 5-3). Chicago won a Wild Card berth over Washington on the basis of best net points in all games (plus 57 net points to plus 53).

First round playoff: HOUSTON 13, Denver 7
Divisional playoffs: Houston 17, SAN DIEGO 14; PITTSBURGH 34, Miami 14
AFC championship: PITTSBURGH 27, Houston 13
First round playoff: PHILADELPHIA 27, Chicago 17
Divisional playoffs: TAMPA BAY 24, Philadelphia 17; Los Angeles 21, DALLAS 19
NFC championship: Los Angeles 9, TAMPA BAY 0
Super Bowl XIV: Pittsburgh (AFC) 31, Los Angeles (NFC) 19, at Rose Bowl, Pasadena, Calif.

1980

In leading the Cleveland Browns to the AFC Central championship, Brian Sipe set club records for passing yardage and touchdown passes. But it wasn't Sipe's statistical feats that made the Browns the NFL's top entertainers in 1980. There was nothing ordinary, mind you, about Sipe's 30 touchdowns or his 4,132 yards, better than Dan Fouts's career record of a year earlier and an NFL record if Fouts himself had not thrown for a staggering 4,715 this time around. (Sipe thus became the third quarterback in NFL history to throw for more than 4,000 yards, joining Joe Namath and Fouts. He finished the season with a league-leading 91.4 passer rating and was named NFL player of the year.)

No, it wasn't Sipe's numbers. It was the way he and the Browns continually chose to wrest victory from their opponents in the closing seconds. For this, coach Sam Rutigliano's club earned the title of Kardiac Kids. Of their 16 games, 13 were decided by seven points or fewer.

Their next-to-last outing of the regular season, however, found the Browns in a role reversal with the Minnesota Vikings. Both clubs needed to win the game to clinch a division championship, and the Vikings did it Browns-style. They scored three times in the last five minutes to win 28-23. As time expired, Minnesota quarterback Tommy Kramer lofted a long pass toward a gathering of Vikings and Browns near the goal line and not far from the sideline. The ball was tipped, then cradled by Vikings wide receiver Ahmad Rashad, who backed into the end zone.

A week later, the Browns became AFC Central champions, defeating Cincinnati 27-24. It was Cleveland's first division championship in nine years. Celebrations were short-lived, however, as the Browns were eliminated in the first round of the AFC playoffs.

Trailing the Oakland Raiders 14-12 on a frozen field in Cleveland, the Browns appeared to be rehearsing for the Super Bowl from their familiar script when Raiders safety Mike Davis stepped in front of Ozzie Newsome in the end zone and intercepted Sipe's third-down pass, thrown with enough time for another play and the ball on the Oakland 13. "I should have thrown it into Lake Erie," Sipe said.

The Raiders won a 34-27 roller coaster of a game against San Diego a week later to take the AFC title, becoming the second wild-card team to reach the Super Bowl. They became the first wild-card team to win it, defeating head coach Dick Vermeil's rejuvenated Philadelphia Eagles 27-10 at the Louisiana Superdome, mostly due to the passing of Jim Plunkett. The former Heisman Trophy winner, written off by New England and later San Francisco in the 1970s, was named the game's most valuable player. Raiders linebacker Rod Martin intercepted three passes from Eagles quarterback Ron Jaworski, providing counterpoint to Plunkett's three touchdown passes.

Vermeil was a minor media phenomenon, having gained a certain measure of notoriety for a work ethic that included spending the night in his office and one time falling asleep in the early morning after having driven his car as far as the driveway.

The Eagles got to New Orleans by taking advantage of eight Minnesota turnovers ("We had twenty-six in the regular season," said Vikings head coach Bud Grant, "so the law of averages had to catch up with us") for a 31-16 first-round victory, then grinding out 263 rushing yards to defeat Dallas 20-7 in the NFC Championship Game.

Of the 224 NFL games played during the 1980 season, one deserves mention for its special place in league history. On December 12, the San Francisco 49ers staged the greatest second-half comeback ever. After trailing the New Orleans Saints 35-7 at intermission, the 49ers came back with four touchdowns and a field goal to win 38-35. By season's end, San Francisco rookie running back Earl Cooper led the NFC in receptions with

Running back Wilbert Montgomery powered the Eagles' offense.

83, and behind him was San Francisco wide receiver Dwight Clark with 82. Were the 49ers sending the league a message?

1980

AMERICAN CONFERENCE

EASTERN DIVISION

	W	L	T	Pct.	Pts.	OP
Buffalo	11	5	0	.688	320	260
New England	10	6	0	.625	441	325
Miami	8	8	0	.500	266	305
Baltimore	7	9	0	.438	355	387
N.Y. Jets	4	12	0	.250	302	395

CENTRAL DIVISION

	W	L	T	Pct.	Pts.	OP
Cleveland	11	5	0	.688	357	310
Houston*	11	5	0	.688	295	251
Pittsburgh	9	7	0	.563	352	313
Cincinnati	6	10	0	.375	244	312

WESTERN DIVISION

	W	L	T	Pct.	Pts.	OP
San Diego	11	5	0	.688	418	327
Oakland*	11	5	0	.688	364	306
Kansas City	8	8	0	.500	319	336
Denver	8	8	0	.500	310	323
Seattle	4	12	0	.250	291	408

NATIONAL CONFERENCE

EASTERN DIVISION

	W	L	T	Pct.	Pts.	OP
Philadelphia	12	4	0	.750	384	222
Dallas*	12	4	0	.750	454	311
Washington	6	10	0	.375	261	293
St. Louis	5	11	0	.313	299	350
N.Y. Giants	4	12	0	.250	249	425

CENTRAL DIVISION

	W	L	T	Pct.	Pts.	OP
Minnesota	9	7	0	.563	317	308
Detroit	9	7	0	.563	334	272
Chicago	7	9	0	.438	304	264
Tampa Bay	5	10	1	.344	271	341
Green Bay	5	10	1	.344	231	371

WESTERN DIVISION

	W	L	T	Pct.	Pts.	OP
Atlanta	12	4	0	.750	405	272
Los Angeles*	11	5	0	.688	424	289
San Francisco	6	10	0	.375	320	415
New Orleans	1	15	0	.063	291	487

**Wild Card qualifier for playoffs*

Philadelphia won division title over Dallas on the basis of best net points in division games (plus 84 net points to plus 50). Minnesota won division title because of a better conference record than Detroit (8-4 to 9-5). Cleveland won division title because of a better conference record than Houston (8-4 to 7-5). San Diego won division title over Oakland on the basis of best net points in division games (plus 60 net points to plus 37).

First round playoff: OAKLAND 27, Houston 7
Divisional playoffs: SAN DIEGO 20, Buffalo 14; Oakland 14, CLEVELAND 12
AFC championship: Oakland 34, SAN DIEGO 27
First round playoff: DALLAS 34, Los Angeles 13
Divisional playoffs: PHILADELPHIA 31, Minnesota 16; Dallas 30, ATLANTA 27
NFC championship: PHILADELPHIA 20, Dallas 7
Super Bowl XV: Oakland (AFC) 27, Philadelphia (NFC) 10, at Louisiana Superdome, New Orleans, La.

1981

Want to take a stab at naming the play of the year? Was it Jack (Hacksaw) Reynolds's tackling Cincinnati fullback Pete Johnson at the 1-foot line on fourth down, the finale of San Francisco's storied goal-line stand in its Super Bowl XVI victory? Or maybe Dan Bunz's tackling running back Charles Alexander at the 1-yard line on the previous down? Or maybe the flea-flicker from Don Strock to Duriel Harris to Tony Nathan that brought Miami to within reach at 24-17 after trailing 24-0 earlier in its classic overtime struggle against San Diego in an AFC Divisional Playoff Game?

Keep nominating. . .but don't leave out Joe Greene's pass completion to a small boy in a dimly lit tunnel. The image of Greene tossing his number 75 Pittsburgh Steelers jersey to the near-speechless kid, which served as the visual tag line to a commercial for Coca-Cola, impressed viewers so strongly that three years later, when a company called Video Storyboard Tests published the results of its annual survey of outstanding TV commercials in *Adweek* magazine, it turned out that viewers identified the spot as the best commercial they had seen in the past *four weeks*.

It wasn't as if the NFL needed a survey to know that its star players had reached a high level of identifiability. When Joe Namath modeled his legs in a pantyhose commercial during the early 1970s, the advertisers had a hit on their hands. Ditto Lite Beer from Miller, "everything you ever wanted in a beer. . .and less," the ideal vehicle for such NFL notables as Dick Butkus, Bubba Smith, John Madden, Bert Jones, and L.C. Greenwood.

Now, what about the 49ers? In a year noted for competitive oddities—such as Oakland's 7-9 fourth-place showing in the AFC West, a mark that included three straight shutout losses—coach Bill Walsh's San Francisco club went 13-3. After brushing aside the New York Giants in the opening round of the playoffs, the 49ers met Dallas at Candlestick Park for the NFC championship. Nine years after "Black Saturday," the 49ers repaid the Cowboys in kind. Add Joe Montana's six-yard touchdown pass to Dwight Clark with 51 seconds remaining to the list of 1981's most memorable plays.

In Super Bowl XVI, the 49ers met Cincinnati, whose "home-field advantage" in the AFC Championship Game had been a record-setting (for both the city of Cincinnati and the NFL) wind-chill factor of minus-59 degrees. It's a good bet no team ever will approach the one-week 130-degree turnaround San Diego experienced between Miami and Cincinnati. On the Chargers' team bus traveling to Riverfront Stadium on game day, head coach Don Coryell jumped up and, pointing to ominous clouds of steam rising from the Ohio River, exhorted his players. "See? See?" he said. "It's not that cold out there." At the time, nobody had the courage to explain the phenomenon: The air temperature was well below the water temperature. The Chargers froze, ultimately losing 27-7.

Sometime during the aftermath, it must have been mentioned, as weak consolation, that Chargers quarterback Dan Fouts had broken his own passing records for a second consecutive year. Fouts's totals: 609 attempts, 360 completions, and 4,802 yards.

Super Bowl XVI took place indoors, in the comfortable Pontiac Silverdome. The salient statistics of the day were Cincinnati quarterback Ken Anderson's Super Bowl-record 25 completions and his teammate Dan Ross's record 11 receptions. But the winning numbers belonged to San Francisco quarterback Montana, honored as the game's most valuable player (14 completions in 22 attempts for 157 yards and one touchdown), and Ray Wersching (a record-tying four field goals and effective squib kickoffs). Numbers aside, major credit for the 49ers' 26-21 victory went to the San Francisco defense.

Just as the 49ers had prefaced their championship year with a proliferation of passing in 1980, the Washington Redskins used 1981 as a stepping stone to something

DEVELOPMENT OF THE UNIFORM

Ken Anderson, Quarterback, Cincinnati Bengals
Modern uniforms have been improved for safety and streamlined for comfort. Helmets have custom-fit, impact-absorbent liners; jerseys are tailored to prevent holding; and air-cushioned "flak jackets" protect ribs.

Wide receiver Dwight Clark made "The Catch," the leaping, end-zone reception that put the 49ers in Super Bowl XVI.

greater. Under new head coach Joe Gibbs, the team began the 1981 season by dropping its first five games. During the week prior to the sixth game, quarterback Joe Theismann, who had drawn criticism for paying too much attention to his restaurant, radio program, and other off-the-field interests, paid an impromptu late-evening visit to a nearby neighbor—Gibbs.

"I just walked up to his house at eleven o'clock at night and knocked on his door," Theismann told Michael Madden in an interview for *PRO!* magazine. "I told him, 'Coach, I think it's time you and I sat down and talked because something's not right, and I'd like to talk to you about it.' I wanted to clarify for him that football was the most important thing in my life."

The following Sunday, the Redskins beat Chicago 24-7. Washington won seven of its remaining 10 games, finishing the season at 8-8. Theismann had the second-highest single-season passing yardage total (3,568) in Washington history. He and the Redskins were ready for 1982.

1981

AMERICAN CONFERENCE

EASTERN DIVISION

	W	L	T	Pct.	Pts.	OP
Miami	11	4	1	.719	345	275
N.Y. Jets*	10	5	1	.656	355	287
Buffalo*	10	6	0	.625	311	276
Baltimore	2	14	0	.125	259	533
New England	2	14	0	.125	322	370

CENTRAL DIVISION

	W	L	T	Pct.	Pts.	OP
Cincinnati	12	4	0	.750	421	304
Pittsburgh	8	8	0	.500	356	297
Houston	7	9	0	.438	281	355
Cleveland	5	11	0	.313	276	375

WESTERN DIVISION

	W	L	T	Pct.	Pts.	OP
San Diego	10	6	0	.625	478	390
Denver	10	6	0	.625	321	289
Kansas City	9	7	0	.563	343	290
Oakland	7	9	0	.438	273	343
Seattle	6	10	0	.375	322	388

NATIONAL CONFERENCE

EASTERN DIVISION

	W	L	T	Pct.	Pts.	OP
Dallas	12	4	0	.750	367	277
Philadelphia*	10	6	0	.625	368	221
N.Y. Giants*	9	7	0	.563	295	257
Washington	8	8	0	.500	347	349
St. Louis	7	9	0	.438	315	408

CENTRAL DIVISION

	W	L	T	Pct.	Pts.	OP
Tampa Bay	9	7	0	.563	315	268
Detroit	8	8	0	.500	397	322
Green Bay	8	8	0	.500	324	361
Minnesota	7	9	0	.438	325	369
Chicago	6	10	0	.375	253	324

WESTERN DIVISION

	W	L	T	Pct.	Pts.	OP
San Francisco	13	3	0	.813	357	250
Atlanta	7	9	0	.438	426	355
Los Angeles	6	10	0	.375	303	351
New Orleans	4	12	0	.250	207	378

**Wild Card qualifier for playoffs*

San Diego won AFC Western title over Denver on the basis of a better division record (6-2 to 5-3). Buffalo won a Wild Card playoff berth over Denver as the result of a 9-7 victory in head-to-head competition.

First round playoff: Buffalo 31, NEW YORK JETS 27

Divisional playoffs: San Diego 41, MIAMI 38, sudden death overtime; CINCINNATI 28, Buffalo 21

AFC championship: CINCINNATI 27, San Diego 7

First round playoff: New York Giants 27, PHILADELPHIA 21

Divisional playoffs: DALLAS 38, Tampa Bay 0; SAN FRANCISCO 38, New York Giants 24

NFC championship: SAN FRANCISCO 28, Dallas 27

Super Bowl XVI: San Francisco (NFC) 26, Cincinnati (AFC) 21, at Silverdome, Pontiac, Mich.

My Favorite Year was the title of a 1982 movie. The movie was not about anyone connected with the NFL.

On May 11, a new pro football league—the United States Football League—was formed, one that would play its games in the springtime starting in 1983.

After two games of the NFL's regular season had been played, a 57-day players strike began on September 22, gouging the schedule with a seven-week void whose impact would reverberate in the coming years. Suddenly, television viewers no longer had the Oilers versus the Saints on Sunday afternoon.

The expiration, on July 15, of the NFL Players Association's contract with the league came amid well-publicized but little-understood NFLPA demands that the players as a group receive 55 percent of the 28 clubs' gross revenues. By the time the strike was settled, that figure virtually had disappeared from all discussions and had dissolved into agreements on such items as higher minimum salaries and a severance pay plan, the first ever in professional sports.

The strike interrupted the first year in Los Angeles for the Raiders, who had defied an NFL rule that forbids moving a franchise without the approval of three-fourths of the clubs.

When post-strike play resumed on November 21, the idea of divisions was temporarily suspended. Instead, playoff bids for a special postseason tournament would go to the top eight teams in the two 14-team conferences. It was agreed that an extra week would be added to the remaining schedule, so that each team would total nine games.

Even with the hiatus, the short season presented pro football with a fair supply of exciting new talent. Kenneth Sims, a 270-pound All-America defensive end from the University of Texas, was the number-one choice in the draft and went to the New England Patriots. Further into the first round, and further than the

Freeman McNeil of the Jets was the NFL's leading rusher.

Los Angeles Raiders expected, USC's Heisman Trophy-winning tailback Marcus Allen still was available. They took him as the tenth pick overall in the draft, and he led the league in touchdowns (14) and points scored (84), finishing fourth in the overall rushing statistics with 697 yards. Versatility, however, was his main value. He also caught 38 passes for 401 yards and three touchdowns. The Raiders' 8-1 record was the American Football Conference's best, and the rookie got his share of the credit.

The Raiders played their first two games on the road, so Los Angeles fans, impatient by nature, were forced to wait more than two months for a look at what they were getting. When it arrived, it looked the same as it had in Oakland. It was Raiders football, all right, Raiders versus Chargers, packaged expressly for a Monday night football presentation from a half-full Los Angeles Memorial Coliseum. San Diego broke on top 24-0, but the Raiders managed a fumble recovery and a quick touchdown just before halftime. Two short touchdown runs by Allen and a clincher by running back Frank Hawkins from one yard out gave the Raiders a 28-24 victory, credibility in L.A., and incredibility in the all-time Monday night standings, which they now led by a mile at 19-2-1.

All San Diego could dredge from the loss was a fact for its 1983 press guide: By passing for 357 yards, Dan Fouts drew even with Johnny Unitas for the all-time career leadership in 300-yard games (26).

Any strike year worth its anguish is going to need some high-quality comic relief. So turn the calendar to December 12. The scene was snow-covered Schaefer (now known as Sullivan) Stadium, home of the Patriots, hosts that afternoon to Miami. In attendance, waiting on the sideline at the wheel of a John Deere 314 tractor, was Mark Henderson, on a one-day work-release leave from Norfolk State Prison. Before the game began, Henderson had helped clear away a layer of snow to make the field halfway playable.

With 4:45 left in a scoreless tie, Patriots placekicker John Smith lined up to try a 33-yard field goal. As New England coach Ron Meyer watched Smith and holder Matt Cavanaugh clearing snow from the kicking area, inspiration struck.

"I looked out on the field," Meyer said, "and I saw John chipping away at the ground, and I thought, 'Let's get the sweeper out there. There's a guy on the sideline who can help us.' "

Henderson did help. Smith hit the field goal. The Patriots won 3-0.

"We told the officials, 'Hey, what's this guy doing?' " said Dolphins nose tackle Bob Baumhower. "They said it was perfectly legal."

A month later, it was perfectly academic, as the Dolphins welcomed the Patriots to round one of the AFC playoffs at the Orange Bowl. Along the sideline, in one corner of the field, someone had piled man-made snow. Next to it was parked a John Deere 314 tractor. The Dolphins, behind a 16-for-19, 246-yard passing performance by David Woodley, eliminated the Patriots 28-13.

A game the day before the snow-plow incident, a continent away and maybe in another galaxy, matched San Diego with San Francisco at Candlestick Park. The Chargers defeated the 49ers 41-37, but if ever a game's drama outweighed its final score, here was that game. San Francisco quarterback Joe Montana dueled with Dan Fouts, and the volley produced an NFL-record 65 complete passes (Montana was 32 for 47 for 366 yards with three touchdowns, Fouts 33 for 48 for 444 yards, the third 400-yard performance of his career, with five touchdowns).

The game was tied twice and had four lead changes, the last coming when Fouts fired the three-yard game-winner to running back Chuck Muncie with 3:22 remaining.

The statistical banquet went on. The combined total yardage came to 1,009. The Chargers' three starting receivers—Wes Chandler, Charlie Joiner, and Kellen Winslow—each had at least 100 yards.

The 16-team postseason festival got underway, and

Running back John Riggins (44) pulled the Redskins' wagon.

the first great drama came in the second round of the AFC playoffs. A crowd of 90,688 packed the Los Angeles Coliseum for what was billed as a "matchup" between Marcus Allen and New York Jets running back Freeman McNeil, the former UCLA star and the league's leading rusher with 786 yards. McNeil won that "battle," outgaining Allen 105-36, but two interceptions by Jets linebacker Lance Mehl in the final two minutes were the game's focal plays, and the Jets won 17-14.

A week later, interceptions knocked the Jets out of the Super Bowl XVII picture, as Miami's "Killer B's" defense, so-called for its abundance of "B" surnames, got a lift from a "D," linebacker A.J. Duhe. In the mud at the Orange Bowl, Duhe intercepted three passes by Richard Todd, returning the third 35 yards for a touchdown, as the Dolphins won 14-0.

Meanwhile, the Washington Redskins—replete with a catalog of group nicknames of their own, such as the Hogs (their enormous offensive line), the Fun Bunch, and a group of receivers so small they were called Smurfs, after the popular kids' toy miniatures—laid waste to NFC postseason foes Detroit (31-7), Minnesota (21-7), and Dallas (31-17).

At the end of January, the Redskins defeated the Dolphins 27-17 at the Rose Bowl in Pasadena, California. Redskins fullback John Riggins, whose four-game postseason rushing yardage, 610, looked odd next to his 553 for the regular season, rushed for a Super Bowl-record 166 yards, including a memorable 43-yard touchdown run on fourth down, and was named the game's most valuable player. "On game days," said Gibbs, "John tells us, 'Hey, just get the wagon out, hitch it up, and I'll pull it. Everybody get on.' "

Had there been an award for most valuable *play*, Joe Theismann would have been the automatic recipient. Noted more for his passing arm, Theismann made a move late in the third quarter that at least qualified as an act of defensive ingenuity, if not valor. With the Redskins trailing 17-13, Theismann's short passing attempt from near his own end zone was batted in the air by Miami's Kim Bokamper. As Bokamper tried to control the ball for an interception that would have given him a clear touchdown, Theismann lunged, got a hand in, and knocked the ball away.

"Very few quarterbacks have the ability or the courage to make that play," Dolphins coach Don Shula said.

Theismann's recollection: "I said, 'Oh, my God.' Then I went for him....I didn't think, I just went. It was the biggest play I made all day."

1982

AMERICAN CONFERENCE

	W	L	T	Pct.	Pts.	OP
L.A. Raiders	8	1	0	.889	260	200
Miami	7	2	0	.778	198	131
Cincinnati	7	2	0	.778	232	177
Pittsburgh	6	3	0	.667	204	146
San Diego	6	3	0	.667	288	221
N.Y. Jets	6	3	0	.667	245	166
New England	5	4	0	.556	143	157
Cleveland	4	5	0	.444	140	182
Buffalo	4	5	0	.444	150	154
Seattle	4	5	0	.444	127	147
Kansas City	3	6	0	.333	176	184
Denver	2	7	0	.222	148	226
Houston	1	8	0	.111	136	245
Baltimore	0	8	1	.056	113	236

NATIONAL CONFERENCE

	W	L	T	Pct.	Pts.	OP
Washington	8	1	0	.889	190	128
Dallas	6	3	0	.667	226	145
Green Bay	5	3	1	.611	226	169
Minnesota	5	4	0	.556	187	198
Atlanta	5	4	0	.556	183	199
St. Louis	5	4	0	.556	135	170
Tampa Bay	5	4	0	.556	158	178
Detroit	4	5	0	.444	181	176
New Orleans	4	5	0	.444	129	160
N.Y. Giants	4	5	0	.444	164	160
San Francisco	3	6	0	.333	209	206
Chicago	3	6	0	.333	141	174
Philadelphia	3	6	0	.333	191	195
L.A. Rams	2	7	0	.222	200	250

As the result of a 57-day players' strike, the 1982 NFL regular season schedule was reduced from 16 weeks to 9. At the conclusion of the regular season, the NFL conducted a 16-team postseason Super Bowl Tournament. Eight teams from each conference were seeded 1-8 based on their records during the season.

Miami finished ahead of Cincinnati based on better conference record (6-1 to 6-2). Pittsburgh won common games tie-breaker with San Diego (3-1 to 2-1) after New York Jets were eliminated from three-way tie based on conference record (Pittsburgh and San Diego 5-3 vs. Jets 2-3). Cleveland finished ahead of Buffalo and Seattle based on better conference record (4-3 to 3-3 to 3-5). Minnesota (4-1), Atlanta (4-3), St. Louis (5-4), Tampa Bay (3-3) seeds were determined by best won-lost record in conference games. Detroit finished ahead of New Orleans and the New York Giants based on better conference record (4-4 to 3-5 to 3-5).

First round playoff: MIAMI 28, New England 13
LOS ANGELES RAIDERS 27, Cleveland 10
New York Jets 44, CINCINNATI 17
San Diego 31, PITTSBURGH 28
Second round playoff: New York Jets 17, LOS ANGELES RAIDERS 14
MIAMI 34, San Diego 13
AFC championship: MIAMI 14, New York Jets 0
First round playoff: WASHINGTON 31, Detroit 7
GREEN BAY 41, St. Louis 16
MINNESOTA 30, Atlanta 24
DALLAS 30, Tampa Bay 17
Second round playoff: WASHINGTON 21, Minnesota 7
DALLAS 37, Green Bay 26
NFC championship: WASHINGTON 31, Dallas 17
Super Bowl XVII: Washington (NFC) 27, Miami (AFC) 17, at Rose Bowl, Pasadena, Calif.

1983

With the prospect of a full season facing them, NFL-watchers focused on youth. They focused too much, perhaps, on one particular youth. Too much, because after the merry-go-round stopped spinning for John Elway, there was no way he'd be living up to all the expectations heaped on his rookie shoulders.

The Colts had the first pick in the draft and made the Stanford quarterback and Heisman runner-up the number-one choice. But Elway had been insisting that he would play only on the West Coast. He even went so far as to sign with the New York Yankees, and he played a season with their Oneonta, New York, farm club.

Shortly after draft day, the Colts turned Denver into a West Coast city, trading Elway to the Broncos for several draft choices and another first-rounder, offensive lineman Chris Hinton of Northwestern. Irony of the year: Elway completed 47.5 percent of his passes for a middling 1,663 yards, tasting only a playoff *hors d'oeuvre* as the Broncos got no further than a loss to Seattle in the AFC Wild Card Game. Hinton, meanwhile, fit perfectly at left guard for the Colts and finished the season as a starter on the AFC Pro Bowl squad.

The first weekend of October, 1983, held a portent of Super Bowl XVIII. In the regular season's fifth week, the Los Angeles Raiders and Washington Redskins hammered away at each other for a full 60 minutes at RFK Stadium. The outcome, 37-35 Redskins, merely whetted the Raiders' appetite for a rematch. There was only one way that could happen this season. . .and the time would come.

Elwaymania in Denver—local television stations set up command posts at the Broncos' training camp—may have blotted out other outstanding newcomers on the NFL landscape, but not for long. Each conference had a rookie running back to ogle. In Los Angeles of the NFC, it was the Rams' Eric Dickerson, chopping into opposing secondaries with his high knees, sprinter's accelera-

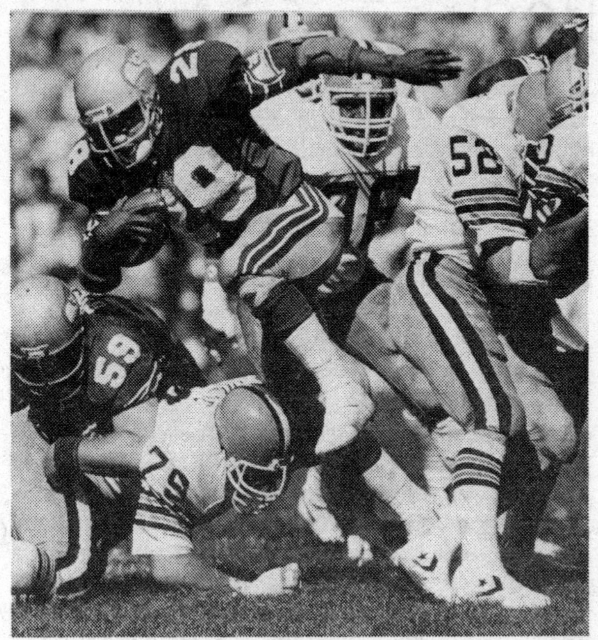

Running back Curt Warner catapulted the Seahawks into AFC championship contention under new head coach Chuck Knox.

tion, and 220 pounds on a 6-foot 3-inch frame. Dickerson led the league in rushing with 1,808 yards, an NFL rookie record.

Next in the overall NFL rushing statistics, but no less valuable to his team, was Seattle's Curt Warner, who amplified new head coach Chuck Knox's tendency to build his offense around the running game. Warner led the AFC with 1,449 yards, running with a see-you-later pivot reminiscent of Hugh McElhenny's swerving forays in the 1950s.

Knox had answered Seattle's call earlier in the year, when the Seahawks were looking to replace Mike McCormack (who replaced Jack Patera), and Knox was having contractual problems in Buffalo. His "Ground

Chuck'' recipe became the Seahawks' main course, supplemented by the new leadership of quarterback Dave Krieg (who replaced veteran Jim Zorn at midseason) and a defense that hit with second-year safety Kenny Easley, a Pro Bowler seemingly from birth. The payoff, in the end, was a trip to the AFC Championship Game.

Seattle gave life to another NFL phenomenon, an activity that soon reached sporting crowds everywhere: The Wave. This new way of getting excited—a vertically shaped undulation of fans standing up, section by section, around and around the stadium—had come over from the University of Washington. No matter; the masses loved it. By 1984, there would be the Triple Wave, the Opposite-Directions Wave, the Silent Wave.

Before round one of the 1983 draft ended, teams had selected no fewer than six quarterbacks. The last of these, and the twenty-seventh man chosen, was University of Pittsburgh quarterback Dan Marino. The Miami Dolphins chose him, and by the end of the 1983 season a lot of clubs wished they'd been as perceptive. Marino's 96.0 passer rating, boosted mainly by a touchdown-passes-to-interceptions ratio of 20-6, led the AFC. The AFC made the rookie quarterback its Pro Bowl starter, although Marino eventually had to forgo the all-star game on account of an ankle injury. What really mattered was that the Dolphins had an offensive mainspring.

New York Jets defensive end Mark Gastineau brought about the beginning of the end for a recent NFL trend: well-rehearsed rubbing it in. Choreographed celebrations had become fashionable among designated groups of players, e.g. the Washington Redskins' ''Fun Bunch,'' which, after one of its members (mostly receivers) scored a touchdown, would form a circle in the end zone, count to three, leap up, and touch hands.

Gastineau was a major contributor to this genre, having developed over the past couple of years something called the ''Sack Dance,'' a frenzied, me-Tarzan, breast-beating, air-punching rampage that lasted a good five or ten seconds after any of Gastineau's quarterback sacks. Fans at Shea Stadium got a big kick out of it. Fans elsewhere showered Gastineau with abuse.

By the time the 1984 season began, rules makers had added "excessive or premeditated celebration by individual players or groups of players" to the list of misdemeanors.

Seattle and the Los Angeles Rams won the AFC and NFC Wild Card Games, the former a 31-7 rout of Denver, the latter a mild 24-17 upset in Dallas. Seattle scored a major upset the following week, knocking over Miami 27-20. The Rams, meanwhile, faced reality in

Quarterback Dan Marino was the AFC's top passer as a rookie.

the form of a 51-7 loss at Washington.

Round one of the NFC bracket gave San Francisco fits. The 49ers survived Detroit's 14-point binge in the fourth quarter, then danced in disbelief as Lions kicker Eddie Murray barely missed a 43-yard field-goal attempt with 11 seconds remaining. San Francisco 24, Detroit 23.

The 49ers were eliminated by a field goal in the NFC Championship Game, as Washington's Mark Moseley kicked a 25-yarder with 40 seconds left to give the Redskins a 24-21 victory and a chance at a second consecutive Super Bowl championship. The Redskins had taken a 21-0 lead into the fourth quarter, but, in a span of slightly more than seven minutes, 49ers quarterback Joe Montana threw three touchdown passes to draw San Francisco even.

The drive toward Moseley's kick was aided by a pair of controversial plays: a pass interference call against 49ers cornerback Eric Wright and a holding penalty against San Francisco's other cornerback, Ronnie Lott.

Meanwhile, the Los Angeles Raiders were rolling comfortably toward Tampa and Super Bowl XVIII with victories over Pittsburgh (38-10) in the first round of the playoffs and Seattle (30-14) for the AFC title. The Seahawks game, played in Los Angeles, attracted a playoff-record crowd of 92,335.

Does the Raiders' 38-9 rout of the Redskins on the NFL's ultimate Sunday call for broad documentation? Some pertinent facts, and one pertinent name, will do: Marcus Allen's record 191 yards rushing, his escape from a *cul-de-sac* for a record 74-yard touchdown run, and his most valuable player award.

John Riggins's anticipated rushing rampage flopped as the Raiders' defensive front penned the Hogs, and Joe Theismann had a tough time locating many open Smurfs.

"We attacked the Hogs and made sure there weren't any running lanes open for Riggins," said Raiders linebacker Rod Martin.

When Raiders managing general partner Al Davis stepped to the CBS microphone to accept the Lombardi Trophy from Commissioner Pete Rozelle, Davis said his thank you, then revealed the full text of his pregame locker room talk:

"Just win, baby."

The year had a midseason epilogue, a hitch in time, a note that doesn't fit a breezy run-through of anecdotes and results. On October 31, George Halas, the last surviving founder of the NFL, died at 88. Player, coach, and owner of the Chicago Bears, "Papa Bear" was the league's patriarch. As Mickey Herskowitz wrote in *PRO!* magazine, "George Halas was chairman of the board, a millionaire, a man who earned everything he got. He was the last of the pioneers. He helped deliver pro football from the sandlots to the super stadiums. His contributions to the sport are beyond measure."

1983

AMERICAN CONFERENCE

EASTERN DIVISION

	W	L	T	Pct.	Pts.	OP
Miami	12	4	0	.750	389	250
New England	8	8	0	.500	274	289
Buffalo	8	8	0	.500	283	351
Baltimore	7	9	0	.438	264	354
N.Y. Jets	7	9	0	.438	313	331

CENTRAL DIVISION

	W	L	T	Pct.	Pts.	OP
Pittsburgh	10	6	0	.625	355	303
Cleveland	9	7	0	.563	356	342
Cincinnati	7	9	0	.438	346	302
Houston	2	14	0	.125	288	460

WESTERN DIVISION

	W	L	T	Pct.	Pts.	OP
L.A. Raiders	12	4	0	.750	442	338
Seattle*	9	7	0	.563	403	397
Denver*	9	7	0	.563	302	327
San Diego	6	10	0	.375	358	462
Kansas City	6	10	0	.375	386	367

NATIONAL CONFERENCE

EASTERN DIVISION

	W	L	T	Pct.	Pts.	OP
Washington	14	2	0	.875	541	332
Dallas*	12	4	0	.750	479	360
St. Louis	8	7	1	.531	374	428
Philadelphia	5	11	0	.313	233	322
N.Y. Giants	3	12	1	.219	267	347

CENTRAL DIVISION

	W	L	T	Pct.	Pts.	OP
Detroit	9	7	0	.563	347	286
Green Bay	8	8	0	.500	429	439
Chicago	8	8	0	.500	311	301
Minnesota	8	8	0	.500	316	348
Tampa Bay	2	14	0	.125	241	380

WESTERN DIVISION

	W	L	T	Pct.	Pts.	OP
San Francisco	10	6	0	.625	432	293
L.A. Rams*	9	7	0	.563	361	344
New Orleans	8	8	0	.500	319	337
Atlanta	7	9	0	.438	370	389

**Wild Card qualifier for playoffs*

Seattle and Denver gained Wild Card berths over Cleveland because of their victories over the Browns.

First round playoff: SEATTLE 31, Denver 7

Divisional playoffs: Seattle 27, MIAMI 20; LOS ANGELES RAIDERS 38, Pittsburgh 10

AFC championship: LOS ANGELES RAIDERS 30, Seattle 14

First round playoff: Los Angeles Rams 24, DALLAS 17

Divisional playoffs: SAN FRANCISCO 24, Detroit 23; WASHINGTON 51, L.A. Rams 7

NFC championship: WASHINGTON 24, San Francisco 21

Super Bowl XVIII: Los Angeles Raiders (AFC) 38, Washington (NFC) 9, at Tampa Stadium, Tampa, Fla.

1984

The mark of any NFL season usually is an amalgam of statistics, off-the-field developments, and individual milestones. Once those have identified themselves, time goes to work on the weaker ones. NFL years wear names. Fast forward, from the Green Bay-Lombardi 1960s. . . . 1968: Namath. 1970: Merger. 1972: Dolphins. 1973: O.J. 1974: Steelers. 1975: Steelers. 1978: Steelers. 1979: Steelers. 1982: Strike.

Then came 1984.

Ominous overtones and overused references to George Orwell's novel aside, this was a year of exaggeration around the NFL. No season in recent memory, in fact no season ever, had matched the epidemic of record-breaking that visited the league. The breakdown:

—Miami quarterback Dan Marino threw 48 touchdown passes, well outdistancing the former single-season record of 36 held by Y.A. Tittle and George Blanda. In the process, Marino also became the first man ever to throw for more than 5,000 yards in one NFL season, finishing with 5,084.

—One of Marino's bullet-like wide receivers, Mark Clayton, caught 18 of those scoring passes, breaking a 23-year-old mark.

—Chicago running back Walter Payton set a new record for career rushing yardage, surpassing Jim Brown's previously sacrosanct standard of 12,312 in early October, and extending his total to 13,309 by season's end.

—Los Angeles Rams running back Eric Dickerson broke O.J. Simpson's single-season rushing record of 2,003 yards, finishing 1984 with 2,105. (Speaking of Dickerson's pace—3,915 yards after only two years in the league—Payton said of his own career total, "I think I'd like to stop if I get to 15,000. But that record won't be safe. The only way I could keep it away from Eric would be to play until I'm forty-three." Payton turns 43 in 1997.)

—Dickerson also broke the record for combined yard-

Chicago's Walter Payton became the all-time rushing leader.

age in one season, breaking Simpson's 1975 total by a single yard with 2,244. Dickerson's 12 games with at least 100 yards rushing surpassed another of O.J.'s marks. The former Buffalo star had done it 11 times in 1973, as had Houston's Earl Campbell in 1979.

—Washington's Art Monk broke the 20-year-old record for receptions in a single season (101) set by Houston's Charley Hennigan in 1964, catching 11 passes in the Redskins' final game against St. Louis to finish with 106 for the year.

—San Diego wide receiver Charlie Joiner topped Charley Taylor's record of 649 career receptions, then extended his total to 657. The 37-year-old veteran of 16 seasons with Houston, Cincinnati, and the Chargers also became the fourth receiver to surpass 10,000 yards, finishing 1984 with 10,774 (in second place behind all-time yardage record-holder Don Maynard's 11,834).

—The Chicago Bears' defense set a single-season record with 72 quarterback sacks, 17½ of which belonged to second-year defensive end Richard Dent, the top total in the NFC.

—The San Francisco 49ers went 15-1 in the regular season, a record for total victories. The 49ers' only loss came at home in week seven against Pittsburgh, a 20-17 setback that nearly reached overtime when Ray Wersching's field-goal attempt sailed wide. The 49ers' 15 victories were one better than the Miami Dolphins' 14 in their perfect 1972 season and the Pittsburgh Steelers' 14 in 1978, when they went on to win Super Bowl XIII.

Eric Dickerson of the Rams rushed for a record 2,105 yards.

—Kansas City placekicker Nick Lowery qualified for consideration in the category of career field-goal accuracy by attempting his 150th three-pointer. Doing so, he became the NFL's all-time leader, with 74.7 percent.

—Tampa Bay running back James Wilder set an all-time record for rushing attempts in a single season, 407. Wilder fell just 15 yards short of Dickerson's record of 2,244 combined rushing and receiving yards.

Postseason activities in the two conferences yielded an intriguing, emotionally charged Super Bowl XIX matchup that seemed ordained from the time the clubs had sorted themselves into the tournament brackets. Miami and its "Marino Corps" strutted through the opening round and the AFC Championship Game with victories over Seattle (31-10) and Pittsburgh (45-28). The Dolphins' mortal moments of 1984 appeared to be well behind them—an overtime loss to San Diego in mid-November and an early-December setback against the Los Angeles Raiders that obscured Marino's best passing effort of the season, 470 yards and four touchdowns.

San Francisco's postseason march was even less charitable than its 15-1 treatment of regular-season opponents. Neither the New York Giants, 21-10 losers in the playoff opener, nor the Chicago Bears, 23-0 losers in the NFC Championship Game, could get a touchdown from their offensive unit. Reporters, electronic and print, came out of the deal with egg on their collective face, having predicted tough times for the 49ers' offense against the league-leading Bears' defense, the alleged heir to the old "Monsters of the Midway" monicker.

If predicting the Super Bowl contestants had been a ho-hum proposition, the pregame discussions and analyses generated an almost pre-thermonuclear climate.

Topic A was Marino. How would the 49ers contain this human cannon, with his stable of speed merchants—Clayton, Mark Duper, *et al*—poised to run the San Francisco secondary out of Stanford Stadium? From there, the conversation might turn, within five minutes, to whether Marino was the greatest of all time.

MVP Joe Montana won Super Bowl XIX's quarterback showdown.

San Francisco quarterback Joe Montana, second-rated in the NFL behind Marino and a good 1,400 yards shorter in the 1984 passing statistics, said, "I think our offense is sort of being overlooked. We may have something to prove."

The 49ers manhandled the Dolphins 38-16, as Montana threw for three touchdowns, rushed for one, and totaled 390 offensive yards for the day, winning Super Bowl MVP honors for the second time in his six-year career. The game also marked a high point in the two-year career of 49ers running back Roger Craig, an all-purpose runner and pass receiver with skills perfectly matched to Bill Walsh's offensive variety show. Craig scored three of the 49ers' touchdowns.

But in the end, it was a defensive gambit that deserved the highest praise. In the face of San Francisco's four-man front, Marino's vision was colored red throughout the afternoon. He was sacked four times for a total of 29 yards. Meanwhile, upfield, San Francisco's five defensive backs, four of them Pro Bowlers, allowed Clayton and Duper a combined total of seven receptions, no touchdowns, and 103 yards.

The 1984 season had another mark, one that came quickly, raised a furor, then took its place in the changing picture of the league. Colts owner Robert Irsay loaded his team's belongings aboard a fleet of moving vans and set out for Indianapolis in the middle of the night. The club's new home would be the 61,000-seat Hoosier Dome, part of an $82-million downtown stadium and convention center.

1984

AMERICAN CONFERENCE

EASTERN DIVISION

	W	L	T	Pct.	Pts.	OP
Miami	14	2	0	.875	513	298
New England	9	7	0	.563	362	352
N.Y. Jets	7	9	0	.438	332	364
Indianapolis	4	12	0	.250	239	414
Buffalo	2	14	0	.125	250	454

CENTRAL DIVISION

	W	L	T	Pct.	Pts.	OP
Pittsburgh	9	7	0	.563	387	310
Cincinnati	8	8	0	.500	339	339
Cleveland	5	11	0	.313	250	297
Houston	3	13	0	.188	240	437

WESTERN DIVISION

	W	L	T	Pct.	Pts.	OP
Denver	13	3	0	.813	353	241
Seattle*	12	4	0	.750	418	282
L.A. Raiders*	11	5	0	.688	368	278
Kansas City	8	8	0	.500	314	324
San Diego	7	9	0	.438	394	413

NATIONAL CONFERENCE

EASTERN DIVISION

	W	L	T	Pct.	Pts.	OP
Washington	11	5	0	.688	426	310
N.Y. Giants*	9	7	0	.563	299	301
St. Louis	9	7	0	.563	423	345
Dallas	9	7	0	.563	308	308
Philadelphia	6	9	1	.406	278	320

CENTRAL DIVISION

	W	L	T	Pct.	Pts.	OP
Chicago	10	6	0	.625	325	248
Green Bay	8	8	0	.500	390	309
Tampa Bay	6	10	0	.375	335	380
Detroit	4	11	1	.281	283	408
Minnesota	3	13	0	.188	276	484

WESTERN DIVISION

	W	L	T	Pct.	Pts.	OP
San Francisco	15	1	0	.938	475	227
L.A. Rams*	10	6	0	.625	346	316
New Orleans	7	9	0	.438	298	361
Atlanta	4	12	0	.250	281	382

**Wild Card qualifier for playoffs*

New York Giants clinched Wild Card berth based on 3-1 record vs. St. Louis's 2-2 and Dallas's 1-3. St. Louis finished ahead of Dallas based on better division record (5-3 to 3-5).

First round playoff: SEATTLE 13, Los Angeles Raiders 7
Divisional playoffs: MIAMI 31, Seattle 10; Pittsburgh 24, DENVER 17
AFC championship: MIAMI 45, Pittsburgh 28
First round playoff: New York Giants 16, LOS ANGELES RAMS 13
Divisional playoffs: SAN FRANCISCO 21, New York Giants 10;
Chicago 23, WASHINGTON 10
NFC championship: SAN FRANCISCO 23, Chicago 0
Super Bowl XIX: San Francisco (NFC) 38, Miami (AFC) 16, at Stanford Stadium, Stanford, Calif.

1985

The Chicago Bears used the 1985 NFL season as a forum to debate the verity of the old sports maxim, "It ain't over 'til it's over." In this case, it was over as soon as it had begun.

There no longer were any doubts that the Monsters of the Midway had returned from a long hibernation. Since former Bears all-pro tight end Mike Ditka had become head coach in 1982, the team had steadily improved from 3-6 to 8-8 to 11-7. Much to the delight of championship-starved hometown fans, the Bears came back snarling from the humiliation of being shut out by the 49ers in the previous season's NFC Championship Game and were taking no prisoners in the new season. The 1985 team was big, strong, fast, deep, well-coached, and, huzzah!, fun. It had personality, collectively, as well as personalities, individually.

One of the most unusual of those personalities belonged to brash fourth-year quarterback Jim McMahon, he of the punk spike haircut, dark glasses, and headbands (more on headbands later). McMahon, gratingly cocky to some, refreshingly so to others, had missed the latter part of the 1984 season after sustaining a lacerated kidney. In the 1985 season opener against Tampa Bay, his first full regular season game since his injury, McMahon served notice to the league that the Bears considered the NFL championship their manifest destiny.

Walter Payton picked up where he had left off in 1984 in his campaign to take over the rushing section of the *NFL Record and Fact Book*. Against the Buccaneers and their new head coach, Leeman Bennett, Payton gained 120 yards on 17 carries, the sixty-fourth 100-yard game of his 11-year NFL career. By season's end, he raised his NFL-record total of 100-yard games to 73, nine of them coming in a record-breaking streak. "Sweetness," who gained 1,551 yards rushing in 1985, also set records with his ninth 1,000-yard season on the ground and third straight 2,000-combined-yard season.

Few defenses dominated the NFL as completely as Chicago's.

Speaking of records, the Chicago defense didn't lose any momentum over the offseason, either. Overcoming the disruption of holdouts by two of the unit's stars, safety Todd Bell and linebacker Al Harris (they never did come to terms and sat out the entire season), the Bears maddening "46" defense dominated the opposition. The 46 was the brainchild of Chicago defensive coordinator Buddy Ryan. There was no big secret to its effectiveness; it simply caused mathematical mismatches by rushing more defenders than there were offensive blockers, and only the Bears knew exactly where those extra rushers were coming from.

At midseason, Chicago was undefeated and Ditka could be credited with creating the media sensation of the season—and maybe the year—in the huge personage of William (The Refrigerator) Perry. Perry, a 300-plus-pound rookie defensive tackle from Clemson, was considered by Ryan a "wasted" draft choice when the Bears took him in the first round. But the youngster proved to be worth his weight in more than just public relations value when Ditka began using him in the offensive backfield in goal-line and short-yardage situations.

The Refrigerator legend got its start in the sixth game of the season, when the Bears dispatched the 49ers with surprising alacrity. Chicago's defense held San Francisco to 11 first downs and 183 yards, both lows in the seven-year tenure of 49ers head coach Bill Walsh. It sacked quarterback Joe Montana seven times, a career high. On top of the indignation of those statistics, Chicago heaped Perry, using him as a running back the last two plays of the game; he gained two yards each carry, one yard more than the 49ers' second-half rushing total.

The next week, in a Monday night victory over Green Bay, Perry lined up at fullback for three goal-line plays in the second quarter. He ran for one touchdown and blasted holes for Payton on two others. Within hours after the game, The Refrigerator was a national celebrity, garnering invitations from the Tonight, Today, and David Letterman shows, along with countless lucrative offers to appear in commercials. Two weeks later, against the Packers again, Perry went in motion from a wingback position and made an over-the-shoulder touchdown catch without breaking stride. Only in America.

The Chicago juggernaut rolled unchecked through Dallas and Atlanta in weeks 11 and 12, where it crushed the Cowboys 44-0 (clinching the NFC Central Division title) and Falcons 36-0 (against whom Perry rushed for another touchdown). Then came Monday night in Miami. The Dolphins did what no other team had been able to do. They beat Chicago 38-24. In the process, Miami protected its distinction as the only perfect-record NFL team ever (17-0 in 1972).

But the Bears were only down momentarily, and not even close to being out. As they sang in the music video the team produced, they were "just here to do the Super Bowl shuffle." Chicago won its last three games, posted the NFL's first same-year back-to-back shutouts in the playoffs against the Giants and Rams, and demolished the New England Patriots 46-10 in the most lopsided Super Bowl victory ever. The Bears took the ball away six times and converted those turnovers into 24 points. They held the AFC champions to a Super Bowl-record low of seven net yards rushing and 123 total yards—four short of the record low. Chicago's 18-1 season record tied the NFL mark for most victories, set by San Francisco in 1984.

McMahon had an outstanding Super Bowl, but defensive end Richard Dent had a great one, too. And symbolizing the entire defense, it was theorized, Dent was named the game's most valuable player.

Nevertheless, McMahon got more than his share of postseason press attention. Much of it stemmed from the Giants playoff game, when he wore a headband with the logo of a sports shoe company, a no-no in the NFL. He was fined by the league office. The next week against the Rams, the same headband was back—around his neck. Around his head, McMahon sported a white headband with "Rozelle" written on it. The Commissioner took it with characteristic aplomb, calling it "a great gag" and saying he wished he had known about it beforehand so that he could have brought out a line of his own athletic shoes. McMahon outdid himself, headband-

Craig James sparked New England's straight-ahead scheme.

wise, in the Super Bowl. He periodically slipped on one of the 25 or so he had with him on the sideline, most bearing the names of charitable organizations.

The Bears didn't get to savor their championship long before the old gang started breaking up. It wasn't wedding bells that did it, it was an offer that defensive mastermind Ryan couldn't refuse. Despite the players pleading with Bears management to do anything to keep him in Chicago, Ryan accepted the head coaching job at Philadelphia, replacing Marion Campbell (who had been fired after the fifteenth game).

(Other head coaches who would not be back in 1986 included: interim coach Wade Phillips at New Orleans, who was replaced by former Baltimore Stars (USFL) head coach Jim Mora; Jim Hanifan at St. Louis, who was replaced by former Dallas assistant Gene Stallings; Hugh Campbell at Houston, who was succeeded by his former defensive coordinator, Jerry Glanville; and Bud Grant, who retired for the second time and was succeeded by his former offensive coordinator, Jerry Burns.)

The Bears, of course, were not the only team to play the 1985 season. It only seemed that way sometimes.

The AFC-champion Patriots had a tremendous year. In Raymond Berry's first complete season as head coach, New England won nine of its last eleven games to get into the playoffs as the conference's second wild-card team, then won three do-or-die postseason victories on the road to qualify for Super Bowl XX.

The Patriots were solid and well-balanced on offense with quarterbacks Tony Eason and Steve Grogan, runnings back Craig James and Tony Collins, wide receivers Stanley Morgan and Irving Fryar, tight end Derrick Ramsey, and bullish linemen John Hannah and Brian Holloway. With linebackers Andre Tippett and Steve Nelson, and cornerbacks Raymond Clayborn and Ronnie Lippett leading an opportunistic, big-play defense, the Patriots turned their brand of basic football into a winning formula.

The team New England defeated in the AFC Cham-

Lionel (Little Train) James loomed large in San Diego's offense.

pionship Game, the Miami Dolphins, had another banner year under coach Don Shula. After sitting out the preseason over a contract dispute, quarterback Dan Marino and his red-hot receiving duo of Mark Clayton and Mark Duper gave another exhibition of aerial pyrotechnics.

The Cleveland Browns also had a dynamite duo on offense. Running backs Earnest Byner (1,002 yards) and rookie Kevin Mack (1,104) made the Browns the third team in NFL history to have two 1,000-yard rushers in the same backfield.

And down in San Diego, Lionel (Little Train) James, the NFL's smallest player at 5 feet 6 inches, set an NFL record with 2,535 all-purpose combined yards. James got his record with a 242-yard performance rushing, receiving, and kick returning against Kansas City in the final game of the season. However, his feat was overshadowed by another amazing performance; Chiefs wide receiver Stephone Paige broke a 40-year-old NFL record with 309 yards, on eight catches.

In the NFC, the New York Giants came of age. Their defense had matured a couple of seasons earlier. But, thanks to quarterback Phil Simms's NFC-leading 3,829 yards passing and the nifty running of another NFL Lilliputian, 5-7 Joe Morris, the offense caught up.

John Robinson's Los Angeles Rams matched Chicago's unbeaten record through the first half of the season. Overcoming a slump following their streak, the Rams gained their first NFC West championship since winning their seventh straight in 1979. Asked what the problem had been in the intervening years, veteran guard Dennis Harrah replied, "The other teams were beating us."

1985

AMERICAN CONFERENCE

EASTERN DIVISION	W	L	T	Pct.	Pts.	OP
Miami	12	4	0	.750	428	320
N.Y. Jets	11	5	0	.688	393	264
New England	11	5	0	.313	320	386
Indianapolis	5	11	0	.313	320	386
Buffalo	2	14	9	.125	200	381
CENTRAL DIVISION	**W**	**L**	**T**	**Pct.**	**Pts.**	**OP**
Cleveland	8	8	0	.500	287	294
Cincinnati	7	9	0	.438	441	437
Pittsburgh	7	9	0	438	379	355
Houston	5	11	0	.313	284	412
WESTERN DIVISION	**W**	**L**	**T**	**Pct.**	**Pts.**	**OP**
L.A. Raiders	12	4	0	.750	354	308
Denver	11	5	0	.688	380	329
Seattle	8	8	0	.500	349	303
San Diego	8	8	0	.500	467	435
Kansas City	6	10	0	.375	327	360

NATIONAL CONFERENCE

EASTERN DIVISION	W	L	T	Pct.	Pts.	OP
Dallas	10	6	0	.625	375	333
N.Y. Giants*	10	6	0	.625	399	283
Washington	10	6	0	.625	298	313
Philadelphia	7	9	0	.438	286	310
St. Louis	5	11	0	.313	279	415
CENTRAL DIVISION	**W**	**L**	**T**	**Pct.**	**Pts.**	**OP**
Chicago	15	1	0	.938	456	198
Green Bay	8	8	0	.500	337	355
Minnesota	7	9	0	.438	346	359
Detroit	7	9	0	.438	307	366
Tampa Bay	2	14	0	.125	294	448
WESTERN DIVISION	**W**	**L**	**T**	**Pct.**	**Pts.**	**OP**
L.A. Rams	11	5	0	.688	340	287
San Francisco*	10	6	0	.625	411	263
New Orleans	5	11	0	.313	294	401
Atlanta	4	12	0	.250	282	452

**Wild Card qualifier for playoffs*

Dallas won division title on better record (3-1) vs. New York Giants (1-3) and Washington (1-3).

New York Jets gained first Wild Card position based on better conference record (9-3) over New England (8-4) and Denver (8-4).

New England gained second Wild Card position based on better record vs. common opponents (4-2) than Denver (3-3).

New York Giants gained first Wild Card position based on better conference record (8-4) over San Francisco (7-5) and Washington (6-6). San Francisco gained second Wild Card position based on head-to-head victory over Washington.

First round playoff: New England 26, NEW YORK JETS 14

Divisional playoffs: MIAMI 24, Cleveland 21; New England 27, LOS ANGELES RAIDERS 20

AFC championship: New England 31, MIAMI 14

First round playoff: NEW YORK GIANTS 17, San Francisco 3

Divisional playoffs: LOS ANGELES RAMS 20, Dallas 0; CHICAGO 21, New York Giants 0

NFC championship: CHICAGO 24, Los Angeles Rams 0

Super Bowl XX: Chicago (NFC) 46, New England (AFC) 10, at Louisiana Superdome, New Orleans, La.

Appendix

Annual Rushing Leaders

Annual Passing Leaders

Annual Pass Receiving Leaders

Annual Interception Leaders

Annual Pro Football
Hall of Fame Inductees

Number-One Draft Choices

ANNUAL RUSHING LEADERS

Year	Player, Team	Att.	Yards	Avg.	TD
1985	Marcus Allen, L.A. Raiders, AFC	380	1,759	4.6	11
	Gerald Riggs, Atlanta, NFC	397	1,719	4.3	10
1984	Eric Dickerson, L.A. Rams, NFC	379	2,105	5.6	14
	Earnest Jackson, San Diego, AFC	296	1,179	4.0	8
1983	*Eric Dickerson, L.A. Rams, NFC	390	1,808	4.6	18
	*Curt Warner, Seattle, AFC	335	1,449	4.3	13
1982	Freeman McNeil, N.Y. Jets, AFC	151	786	5.2	6
	Tony Dorsett, Dallas, NFC	177	745	4.2	5
1981	*George Rogers, New Orleans, NFC	378	1,674	4.4	13
	Earl Campbell, Houston, AFC	361	1,376	3.8	10
1980	Earl Campbell, Houston, AFC	373	1,934	5.2	13
	Walter Payton, Chicago, NFC	317	1,460	4.6	6
1979	Earl Campbell, Houston, AFC	368	1,697	4.6	19
	Walter Payton, Chicago, NFC	369	1,610	4.4	14
1978	*Earl Campbell, Houston, AFC	302	1,450	4.8	13
	Walter Payton, Chicago, NFC	333	1,395	4.2	11
1977	Walter Payton, Chicago, NFC	339	1,852	5.5	14
	Mark van Eeghen, Oakland, AFC	324	1,273	3.9	7
1976	O.J. Simpson, Buffalo, AFC	290	1,503	5.2	8
	Walter Payton, Chicago, NFC	311	1,390	4.5	13
1975	O.J. Simpson, Buffalo, AFC	329	1,817	5.5	16
	Jim Otis, St. Louis, NFC	269	1,076	4.0	5
1974	Otis Armstrong, Denver, AFC	263	1,407	5.3	9
	Lawrence McCutcheon, Los Angeles, NFC	236	1,109	4.7	3
1973	O.J. Simpson, Buffalo, AFC	332	2,003	6.0	12
	John Brockington, Green Bay, NFC	265	1,144	4.3	3
1972	O.J. Simpson, Buffalo, AFC	292	1,251	4.3	6
	Larry Brown, Washington, NFC	285	1,216	4.3	8
1971	Floyd Little, Denver, AFC	284	1,133	4.0	6
	*John Brockington, Green Bay, NFC	216	1,105	5.1	4
1970	Larry Brown, Washington, NFC	237	1,125	4.7	5
	Floyd Little, Denver, AFC	209	901	4.3	3
1969	Gale Sayers, Chicago, NFL	236	1,032	4.4	8
	Dickie Post, San Diego, AFL	182	873	4.8	6
1968	Leroy Kelly, Cleveland, NFL	248	1,239	5.0	16
	*Paul Robinson, Cincinnati, AFL	238	1,023	4.3	8
1967	Jim Nance, Boston, AFL	269	1,216	4.5	7
	Leroy Kelly, Cleveland, NFL	235	1,205	5.1	11
1966	Jim Nance, Boston, AFL	299	1,458	4.9	11
	Gale Sayers, Chicago, NFL	229	1,231	5.4	8
1965	Jim Brown, Cleveland, NFL	289	1,544	5.3	17
	Paul Lowe, San Diego, AFL	222	1,121	5.0	7
1964	Jim Brown, Cleveland, NFL	280	1,446	5.2	7
	Cookie Gilchrist, Buffalo, AFL	230	981	4.3	6
1963	Jim Brown, Cleveland, NFL	291	1,863	6.4	12
	Clem Daniels, Oakland, AFL	215	1,099	5.1	3
1962	Jim Taylor, Green Bay, NFL	272	1,474	5.4	19
	*Cookie Gilchrist, Buffalo, AFL	214	1,096	5.1	13
1961	Jim Brown, Cleveland, NFL	305	1,408	4.6	8
	Billy Cannon, Houston, AFL	200	948	4.7	6
1960	Jim Brown, Cleveland, NFL	215	1,257	5.8	9
	*Abner Haynes, Dall. Texans, AFL	156	875	5.6	9
1959	Jim Brown, Cleveland	290	1,329	4.6	14
1958	Jim Brown, Cleveland	257	1,527	5.9	17
1957	*Jim Brown, Cleveland	202	942	4.7	9
1956	Rick Casares, Chi. Bears	234	1,126	4.8	12
1955	*Alan Ameche, Baltimore	213	961	4.5	9
1954	Joe Perry, San Francisco	173	1,049	6.1	8

Los Angeles Raiders running back Marcus Allen

1953	Joe Perry, San Francisco	192	1,018	5.3	10
1952	Dan Towler, Los Angeles	156	894	5.7	10
1951	Eddie Price, N.Y. Giants	271	971	3.6	7
1950	*Marion Motley, Cleveland	140	810	5.8	3
1949	Steve Van Buren, Philadelphia	263	1,146	4.4	11
1948	Steve Van Buren, Philadelphia	201	945	4.7	10
1947	Steve Van Buren, Philadelphia	217	1,008	4.6	13
1946	Bill Dudley, Pittsburgh	146	604	4.1	3
1945	Steve Van Buren, Philadelphia	143	832	5.8	15
1944	Bill Paschal, N.Y. Giants	196	737	3.8	9
1943	*Bill Paschal, N.Y. Giants	147	572	3.9	10
1942	*Bill Dudley, Pittsburgh	162	696	4.3	5
1941	Clarence (Pug) Manders, Brooklyn	111	486	4.4	5
1940	Byron (Whizzer) White, Detroit	146	514	3.5	5
1939	*Bill Osmanski, Chicago	121	699	5.8	7
1938	*Byron (Whizzer) White, Pittsburgh	152	567	3.7	4
1937	Cliff Battles, Washington	216	874	4.0	5
1936	*Alphonse (Tuffy) Leemans, N.Y. Giants	206	830	4.0	2
1935	Doug Russell, Chi. Cardinals	140	499	3.6	0
1934	*Beattie Feathers, Chi. Bears	101	1,004	9.9	8
1933	Jim Musick, Boston	173	809	4.7	5
1932	*Cliff Battles, Boston	148	576	3.9	3

**First year in the league.*

ANNUAL PASSING LEADERS

Year	Player, Team	Att.	Comp.	Yards	TD	Int.
1985	Dan Marino, Miami, AFC	567	336	4,137	30	21
	Phil Simms, N.Y. Giants, NFC	495	275	3,829	22	20
1984	Dan Marino, Miami, AFC	564	362	5,084	48	17
	Joe Montana, San Francisco, NFC	432	279	3,630	28	10
1983	Steve Bartkowski, Atlanta, NFC	432	274	3,167	22	5
	*Dan Marino, Miami, AFC	296	173	2,210	20	6
1982	Ken Anderson, Cincinnati, AFC	309	218	2,495	12	9
	Joe Theismann, Washington, NFC	252	161	2,033	13	9
1981	Ken Anderson, Cincinnati, AFC	479	300	3,754	29	10
	Joe Montana, San Francisco, NFC	488	311	3,565	19	12
1980	Brian Sipe, Cleveland, AFC	554	337	4,132	30	14
	Ron Jaworski, Philadelphia, NFC	451	257	3,529	27	12
1979	Roger Staubach, Dallas, NFC	461	267	3,586	27	11
	Dan Fouts, San Diego, AFC	530	332	4,082	24	24
1978	Roger Staubach, Dallas, NFC	413	231	3,190	25	16
	Terry Bradshaw, Pittsburgh, AFC	368	207	2,915	28	20
1977	Bob Griese, Miami, AFC	307	180	2,252	22	13
	Roger Staubach, Dallas, NFC	361	210	2,620	18	9
1976	Ken Stabler, Oakland, AFC	291	194	2,737	27	17
	James Harris, Los Angeles, NFC	158	91	1,460	8	6
1975	Ken Anderson, Cincinnati, AFC	377	228	3,169	21	11

New York Giants quarterback Phil Simms

	Fran Tarkenton, Minnesota, NFC	425	273	2,994	25	13
1974	Ken Anderson, Cincinnati, AFC	328	213	2,667	18	10
	Sonny Jurgensen, Washington, NFC	167	107	1,185	11	5
1973	Roger Staubach, Dallas, NFC	286	179	2,428	23	15
	Ken Stabler, Oakland, AFC	260	163	1,997	14	10
1972	Norm Snead, N.Y. Giants, NFC	325	196	2,307	17	12
	Earl Morrall, Miami, AFC	150	83	1,360	11	7
1971	Roger Staubach, Dallas, NFC	211	126	1,882	15	4
	Bob Griese, Miami, AFC	263	145	2,089	19	9
1970	John Brodie, San Francisco, NFC	378	223	2,941	24	10
	Daryle Lamonica, Oakland, AFC	356	179	2,516	22	15
1969	Sonny Jurgensen, Washington, NFL	442	274	3,102	22	15
	*Greg Cook, Cincinnati, AFL	197	106	1,854	15	11
1968	Len Dawson, Kansas City, AFL	224	131	2,109	17	9
	Earl Morrall, Baltimore, NFL	317	182	2,909	26	17
1967	Sonny Jurgensen, Washington, NFL	508	288	3,747	31	16
	Daryle Lamonica, Oakland, AFL	425	220	3,228	30	20
1966	Bart Starr, Green Bay, NFL	251	156	2,257	14	3
	Len Dawson, Kansas City, AFL	284	159	2,527	26	10
1965	Rudy Bukich, Chicago, NFL	312	176	2,641	20	9
	John Hadl, San Diego, AFL	348	174	2,798	20	21
1964	Len Dawson, Kansas City, AFL	354	199	2,879	30	18
	Bart Starr, Green Bay, NFL	272	163	2,144	15	4
1963	Y.A. Tittle, N.Y. Giants, NFL	367	221	3,145	36	14
	Tobin Rote, San Diego, AFL	286	170	2,510	20	17
1962	Len Dawson, Dall. Texans, AFL	310	189	2,759	29	17
	Bart Starr, Green Bay, NFL	285	178	2,438	12	9
1961	George Blanda, Houston, AFL	362	187	3,330	36	22
	Milt Plum, Cleveland, NFL	302	177	2,416	18	10
1960	Milt Plum, Cleveland, NFL	250	151	2,297	21	5
	Jack Kemp, L.A. Chargers, AFL	406	211	3,018	20	25
1959	Charlie Conerly, N.Y. Giants	194	113	1,706	14	4
1958	Eddie LeBaron, Washington	145	79	1,365	11	10
1957	Tommy O'Connell, Cleveland	110	63	1,229	9	8
1956	Ed Brown, Chi. Bears	168	96	1,667	11	12
1955	Otto Graham, Cleveland	185	98	1,721	15	8
1954	Norm Van Brocklin, Los Angeles	260	139	2,637	13	21
1953	Otto Graham, Cleveland	258	167	2,722	11	9
1952	Norm Van Brocklin, Los Angeles	205	113	1,736	14	17
1951	Bob Waterfield, Los Angeles	176	88	1,566	13	10
1950	Norm Van Brocklin, Los Angeles	233	127	2,061	18	14
1949	Sammy Baugh, Washington	255	145	1,903	18	14
1948	Tommy Thompson, Philadelphia	246	141	1,965	25	11
1947	Sammy Baugh, Washington	354	210	2,938	25	15
1946	Bob Waterfield, Los Angeles	251	127	1,747	18	17
1945	Sammy Baugh, Washington	182	128	1,669	11	4
	Sid Luckman, Chi. Bears	217	117	1,725	14	10
1944	Frank Filchock, Washington	147	84	1,139	13	9
1943	Sammy Baugh, Washington	239	133	1,754	23	19
1942	Cecil Isbell, Green Bay	268	146	2,021	24	14
1941	Cecil Isbell, Green Bay	206	117	1,479	15	11
1940	Sammy Baugh, Washington	177	111	1,367	12	10
1939	*Parker Hall, Cleveland	208	106	1,227	9	13
1938	Ed Danowski, N.Y. Giants	129	70	848	7	8
1937	*Sammy Baugh, Washington	171	81	1,127	8	14
1936	Arnie Herber, Green Bay	173	77	1,239	11	13
1935	Ed Danowski, N.Y. Giants	113	57	794	10	9
1934	Arnie Herber, Green Bay	115	42	799	8	12
1933	*Harry Newman, N.Y. Giants	136	53	973	11	17
1932	Arnie Herber, Green Bay	101	37	639	9	9

**First year in the league.*

ANNUAL PASS RECEIVING LEADERS

Year	Player, Team	No.	Yards	Avg.	TD
1985	Roger Craig, San Francisco, NFC	92	1,016	11.0	6
	Lionel James, San Diego, AFC	86	1,027	11.9	6
1984	Art Monk, Washington, NFC	106	1,372	12.9	7
	Ozzie Newsome, Cleveland, AFC	89	1,001	11.2	5
1983	Todd Christensen, L.A. Raiders, AFC	92	1,247	13.6	12
	Roy Green, St. Louis, NFC	78	1,227	15.7	14
	Charlie Brown, Washington, NFC	78	1,225	15.7	8
	Earnest Gray, N.Y. Giants, NFC	78	1,139	14.6	5
1982	Dwight Clark, San Francisco, NFC	60	913	15.2	5
	Kellen Winslow, San Diego, AFC	54	721	13.4	6
1981	Kellen Winslow, San Diego, AFC	88	1,075	12.2	10
	Dwight Clark, San Francisco, NFC	85	1,105	13.0	4
1980	Kellen Winslow, San Diego, AFC	89	1,290	14.5	9
	*Earl Cooper, San Francisco, NFC	83	567	6.8	4
1979	Joe Washington, Baltimore, AFC	82	750	9.1	3
	Ahmad Rashad, Minnesota, NFC	80	1,156	14.5	9
1978	Rickey Young, Minnesota, NFC	88	704	8.0	5
	Steve Largent, Seattle, AFC	71	1,168	16.5	8
1977	Lydell Mitchell, Baltimore, AFC	71	620	8.7	4
	Ahmad Rashad, Minnesota, NFC	51	681	13.4	2
1976	MacArthur Lane, Kansas City, AFC	66	686	10.4	1
	Drew Pearson, Dallas, NFC	58	806	13.9	6
1975	Chuck Foreman, Minnesota, NFC	73	691	9.5	9
	Reggie Rucker, Cleveland, AFC	60	770	12.8	3
	Lydell Mitchell, Baltimore, AFC	60	544	9.1	4
1974	Lydell Mitchell, Baltimore, AFC	72	544	7.6	2
	Charles Young, Philadelphia, NFC	63	696	11.0	3
1973	Harold Carmichael, Philadelphia, NFC	67	1,116	16.7	9
	Fred Willis, Houston, AFC	57	371	6.5	1
1972	Harold Jackson, Philadelphia, NFC	62	1,048	16.9	4
	Fred Biletnikoff, Oakland, AFC	58	802	13.8	7
1971	Fred Biletnikoff, Oakland, AFC	61	929	15.2	9
	Bob Tucker, N.Y. Giants, NFC	59	791	13.4	4
1970	Dick Gordon, Chicago, NFC	71	1,026	14.5	13
	Marlin Briscoe, Buffalo, AFC	57	1,036	18.2	8
1969	Dan Abramowicz, New Orleans, NFL	73	1,015	13.9	7
	Lance Alworth, San Diego, AFL	64	1,003	15.7	4
1968	Clifton McNeil, San Francisco, NFL	71	994	14.0	7
	Lance Alworth, San Diego, AFL	68	1,312	19.3	10
1967	George Sauer, N.Y. Jets, AFL	75	1,189	15.9	6
	Charley Taylor, Washington, NFL	70	990	14.1	9
1966	Lance Alworth, San Diego, AFL	73	1,383	18.9	13
	Charley Taylor, Washington, NFL	72	1,119	15.5	12
1965	Lionel Taylor, Denver, AFL	85	1,131	13.3	6
	Dave Parks, San Francisco, NFL	80	1,344	16.8	12
1964	Charley Hennigan, Houston, AFL	101	1,546	15.3	8
	Johnny Morris, Chicago, NFL	93	1,200	12.9	10
1963	Lionel Taylor, Denver, AFL	78	1,101	14.1	10
	Bobby Joe Conrad, St. Louis, NFL	73	967	13.2	10
1962	Lionel Taylor, Denver, AFL	77	908	11.8	4
	Bobby Mitchell, Washington, NFL	72	1,384	19.2	11
1961	Lionel Taylor, Denver, AFL	100	1,176	11.8	4
	Jim (Red) Phillips, Los Angeles, NFL	78	1,092	14.0	5
1960	Lionel Taylor, Denver, AFL	92	1,235	13.4	12
	Raymond Berry, Baltimore, NFL	74	1,298	17.5	10
1959	Raymond Berry, Baltimore	66	959	14.5	14
1958	Raymond Berry, Baltimore	56	794	14.2	9
	Pete Retzlaff, Philadelphia	56	766	13.7	2

1957	Billy Wilson, San Francisco	52	757	14.6	6
1956	Billy Wilson, San Francisco	60	889	14.8	5
1955	Pete Pihos, Philadelphia	62	864	13.9	7
1954	Pete Pihos, Philadelphia	60	872	14.5	10
	Billy Wilson, San Francisco	60	830	13.8	5
1953	Pete Pihos, Philadelphia	63	1,049	16.7	10
1952	Mac Speedie, Cleveland	62	911	14.7	5
1951	Elroy (Crazylegs) Hirsch, Los Angeles	66	1,495	22.7	17
1950	Tom Fears, Los Angeles	84	1,116	13.3	7
1949	Tom Fears, Los Angeles	77	1,013	13.2	9
1948	*Tom Fears, Los Angeles	51	698	13.7	4
1947	Jim Keane, Chi. Bears	64	910	14.2	10
1946	Jim Benton, Los Angeles	63	981	15.6	6
1945	Don Hutson, Green Bay	47	834	17.7	9
1944	Don Hutson, Green Bay	58	866	14.9	9
1943	Don Hutson, Green Bay	47	776	16.5	11
1942	Don Hutson, Green Bay	74	1,211	16.4	17
1941	Don Hutson, Green Bay	58	738	12.7	10
1940	*Don Looney, Philadelphia	58	707	12.2	4
1939	Don Hutson, Green Bay	34	846	24.9	6
1938	Gaynell Tinsley, Chi. Cardinals	41	516	12.6	1
1937	Don Hutson, Green Bay	41	552	13.5	7
1936	Don Hutson, Green Bay	34	536	15.8	8
1935	*Tod Goodwin, N.Y. Giants	26	432	16.6	4
1934	Joe Carter, Philadelphia	16	238	14.9	4
	Morris (Red) Badgro, N.Y. Giants	16	206	12.9	1
1933	John (Shipwreck) Kelly, Brooklyn	22	246	11.2	3
1932	Ray Flaherty, N.Y. Giants	21	350	16.7	3

**First year in the league.*

San Francisco 49ers running back Roger Craig

ANNUAL INTERCEPTION LEADERS

Year	Player, Team	No.	Yards	TD
1985	Everson Walls, Dallas, NFC	9	31	0
	Albert Lewis, Kansas City, AFC	8	59	0
	Eugene Daniel, Indianapolis, AFC	8	53	0
1984	Ken Easley, Seattle, AFC	10	126	2
	*Tom Flynn, Green Bay, NFC	9	106	0
1983	Mark Murphy, Washington, NFC	9	127	0
	Ken Riley, Cincinnati, AFC	8	89	2
	Vann McElroy, L.A. Raiders, AFC	8	68	0
1982	Everson Walls, Dallas, NFC	7	61	0
	Ken Riley, Cincinnati, AFC	5	88	1
	Bobby Jackson, N.Y. Jets, AFC	5	84	1
	Dwayne Woodruff, Pittsburgh, AFC	5	53	0
	Donnie Shell, Pittsburgh, AFC	5	27	0
1981	*Everson Walls, Dallas, NFC	11	133	0
	John Harris, Seattle, AFC	10	155	2
1980	Lester Hayes, Oakland, AFC	13	273	1
	Nolan Cromwell, Los Angeles, NFC	8	140	1
1979	Mike Reinfeldt, Houston, AFC	12	205	0
	Lemar Parrish, Washington, NFC	9	65	0
1978	Thom Darden, Cleveland, AFC	10	200	0
	Ken Stone, St. Louis, NFC	9	139	0
	Willie Buchanon, Green Bay, NFC	9	93	1
1977	Lyle Blackwood, Baltimore, AFC	10	163	0
	Rolland Lawrence, Atlanta, NFC	7	138	0
1976	Monte Jackson, Los Angeles, NFC	10	173	3
	Ken Riley, Cincinnati, AFC	9	141	1
1975	Mel Blount, Pittsburgh, AFC	11	121	0
	Paul Krause, Minnesota, NFC	10	201	0
1974	Emmitt Thomas, Kansas City, AFC	12	214	2
	Ray Brown, Atlanta, NFC	8	164	1
1973	Dick Anderson, Miami, AFC	8	163	2
	Mike Wagner, Pittsburgh, AFC	8	134	0
	Bobby Bryant, Minnesota, NFC	7	105	1

Dallas Cowboys cornerback Everson Walls

1972	Bill Bradley, Philadelphia, NFC	9	73	0
	Mike Sensibaugh, Kansas City, AFC	8	65	0
1971	Bill Bradley, Philadelphia, NFC	11	248	0
	Ken Houston, Houston, AFC	9	220	4
1970	Johnny Robinson, Kansas City, AFC	10	155	0
	Dick LeBeau, Detroit, NFC	9	96	0
1969	Mel Renfro, Dallas, NFL	10	118	0
	Emmitt Thomas, Kansas City, AFL	9	146	1
1968	Dave Grayson, Oakland, AFL	10	195	1
	Willie Williams, N.Y. Giants, NFL	10	103	0
1967	Miller Farr, Houston, AFL	10	264	3
	*Lem Barney, Detroit, NFL	10	232	3
	Tom Janik, Buffalo, AFL	10	222	2
	Dave Whitsell, New Orleans, NFL	10	178	2
	Dick Westmoreland, Miami, AFL	10	127	1
1966	Larry Wilson, St. Louis, NFL	10	180	2
	Johnny Robinson, Kansas City, AFL	10	136	1
	Bobby Hunt, Kansas City, AFL	10	113	0
1965	W.K. Hicks, Houston, AFL	9	156	0
	Bobby Boyd, Baltimore, NFL	9	78	1
1964	Dainard Paulson, N.Y. Jets, AFL	12	157	1
	*Paul Krause, Washington, NFL	12	140	1
1963	Fred Glick, Houston, AFL	12	180	1
	Dick Lynch, N.Y. Giants, NFL	9	251	3
	Roosevelt Taylor, Chicago, NFL	9	172	1
1962	Lee Riley, N.Y. Titans, AFL	11	122	0
	Willie Wood, Green Bay, NFL	9	132	0
1961	Billy Atkins, Buffalo, AFL	10	158	0
	Dick Lynch, N.Y. Giants, NFL	9	60	0
1960	*Austin (Goose) Gonsoulin, Denver, AFL	11	98	0
	Dave Baker, San Francisco, NFL	10	96	0
	Jerry Norton, St. Louis, NFL	10	96	0
1959	Dean Derby, Pittsburgh	7	127	0
	Milt Davis, Baltimore	7	119	1
	Don Shinnick, Baltimore	7	70	0
1958	Jim Patton, N.Y. Giants	11	183	0
1957	*Milt Davis, Baltimore	10	219	2
	Jack Christiansen, Detroit	10	137	1
	Jack Butler, Pittsburgh	10	85	0
1956	Lindon Crow, Chi. Cardinals	11	170	0
1955	Will Sherman, Los Angeles	11	101	0
1954	Dick (Night Train) Lane, Chi. Cardinals	10	181	0
1953	Jack Christiansen, Detroit	12	238	1
1952	*Dick (Night Train) Lane, Los Angeles	14	298	2
1951	Otto Schnellbacher, N.Y. Giants	11	194	2
1950	*Orban (Spec) Sanders, N.Y. Yanks	13	199	0
1949	Bob Nussbaumer, Chi. Cardinals	12	157	0
1948	*Dan Sandifer, Washington	13	258	2
1947	Frank Reagan, N.Y. Giants	10	203	0
	Frank Seno, Boston	10	100	0
1946	Bill Dudley, Pittsburgh	10	242	1
1945	Roy Zimmerman, Philadelphia	7	90	0
1944	*Howard Livingston, N.Y. Giants	9	172	1
1943	Sammy Baugh, Washington	11	112	0
1942	*Clyde (Bulldog) Turner, Chi. Bears	8	96	1
1941	Marshall Goldberg, Chi. Cardinals	7	54	0
	*Art Jones, Pittsburgh	7	35	0
1940	Clarence (Ace) Parker, Brooklyn	6	146	1
	Kent Ryan, Detroit	6	65	0
	Don Hutson, Green Bay	6	24	0

**First year in the league.*

ANNUAL PRO FOOTBALL HALL OF FAME INDUCTEES

1986 **PAUL HORNUNG,** Halfback-Kicker, Green Bay Packers 1957-1962, 1964-66

KEN HOUSTON, Safety, Houston Oilers 1967-1972, Washington Redskins 1973-1980

WILLIE LANIER, Linebacker, Kansas City Chiefs 1967-1977

FRAN TARKENTON, Quarterback, Minnesota Vikings 1961-66, 1972-78; N.Y. Giants 1967-1971

DOAK WALKER, Halfback-Kicker, Detroit Lions 1950-55

1985 **FRANK GATSKI,** Center, Cleveland Browns (AAFC) 1946-49; Cleveland Browns 1950-56; Detroit Lions 1957

JOE NAMATH, Quarterback, N.Y. Jets 1965-1976; L.A. Rams 1977

Paul Hornung

Ken Houston

Doak Walker

Willie Lanier

Fran Tarkenton

PETE ROZELLE, NFL Commissioner 1960-present
O.J. SIMPSON, Running Back, Buffalo Bills 1969-1977; San Francisco 49ers 1978-79
ROGER STAUBACH, Quarterback, Dallas Cowboys 1969-1979

1984 **WILLIE BROWN,** Defensive Back, Denver Broncos 1963-66; Oakland Raiders 1967-1978
MIKE McCORMACK, Offensive Tackle, N.Y. Yankees 1951; Cleveland Browns 1954-1962
CHARLEY TAYLOR, Wide Receiver-Running Back, Washington Redskins 1964-1975, 1977
ARNIE WEINMEISTER, Defensive Tackle, N.Y. Yankees (AAFC) 1948-49; N.Y. Giants 1950-53

1983 **BOBBY BELL,** Linebacker, Kansas City Chiefs 1963-1974
SID GILLMAN, Coach, L.A. Rams 1955-59; L.A. Chargers 1960; San Diego Chargers 1961-69, 1971; Houston Oilers 1973-74
SONNY JURGENSEN, Quarterback, Philadelphia Eagles 1957-1963; Washington Redskins 1964-1974
BOBBY MITCHELL, Running Back-Wide Receiver, Cleveland Browns 1958-1961; Washington Redskins 1962-68
PAUL WARFIELD, Wide Receiver, Cleveland Browns 1964-69, 1976-77; Miami Dolphins 1970-74; Memphis Grizzlies (WFL) 1975

1982 **DOUG ATKINS,** Defensive End, Cleveland Browns 1953-54; Chicago Bears 1955-1966; New Orleans Saints 1967-69
SAM HUFF, Linebacker, N.Y. Giants 1956-1963; Washington Redskins 1964-67, 1969
GEORGE MUSSO, Guard, Chicago Bears 1933-1944
MERLIN OLSEN, Defensive Tackle, L.A. Rams 1962-1976

1981 **MORRIS (RED) BADGRO,** End, N.Y. Yankees 1927; N.Y. Giants 1930-35; Brooklyn Dodgers 1936
GEORGE BLANDA, Quarterback-Kicker, Chicago Bears 1949-1958; Baltimore Colts 1950; Houston Oilers 1960-66; Oakland Raiders 1967-1975
WILLIE DAVIS, Defensive End, Cleveland Browns 1958-59; Green Bay Packers 1960-69
JIM RINGO, Center, Green Bay Packers 1953-1963; Philadelphia Eagles 1964-67

1980 **HERB ADDERLEY,** Defensive Back, Green Bay Packers 1961-69; Dallas Cowboys 1970-72
DAVID (DEACON) JONES, Defensive End, L.A. Rams 1961-1971; San Diego Chargers 1972-73; Washington Redskins 1974
BOB LILLY, Defensive Tackle, Dallas Cowboys 1961-1974
JIM OTTO, Center, Oakland Raiders 1960-1974

1979 **DICK BUTKUS,** Linebacker, Chicago Bears 1965-1973
YALE LARY, Defensive Back-Punter, Detroit Lions 1952-53, 1956-1964
RON MIX, Tackle, San Diego Chargers 1960-69; Oakland Raiders 1971
JOHNNY UNITAS, Quarterback, Baltimore Colts 1956-1972; San Diego Chargers 1973

1978 **LANCE ALWORTH,** Wide Receiver, San Diego Chargers 1962-1970; Dallas Cowboys 1971-72
WEEB EWBANK, Coach, Baltimore Colts 1954-1962; N.Y. Jets 1963-1973
ALPHONSE (TUFFY) LEEMANS, Fullback, N.Y. Giants 1936-1943
RAY NITSCHKE, Linebacker, Green Bay Packers 1958-1972
LARRY WILSON, Defensive Back, St. Louis Cardinals 1960-1972

1977 **FRANK GIFFORD,** Halfback, N.Y. Giants 1952-1960, 1962-64

FORREST GREGG, Tackle, Green Bay Packers 1956, 1958-1970; Dallas Cowboys 1971
GALE SAYERS, Running Back, Chicago Bears 1965-1971
BART STARR, Quarterback, Green Bay Packers 1956-1971
BILL WILLIS, Guard, Cleveland Browns (AAFC) 1946-49; Cleveland Browns 1950-53

1976 **RAY FLAHERTY,** End-Coach, L.A. Wildcats (AFL) 1927-28; N.Y. Yankees 1927; N.Y. Giants 1928-29, 1931-35; coach, Boston Redskins 1936; Washington Redskins 1937-1942; N.Y. Yankees (AAFC) 1946-48; Chicago Hornets (AAFC) 1949
LEN FORD, End, L.A. Dons (AAFC) 1948-49; Cleveland Browns 1950-57; Green Bay Packers 1958
JIM TAYLOR, Fullback, Green Bay Packers 1958-1966; New Orleans Saints 1967

1975 **ROOSEVELT BROWN,** Tackle, N.Y. Giants 1953-1965
GEORGE CONNOR, Tackle-Linebacker, Chicago Bears 1948-1955
DANTE LAVELLI, End, Cleveland Browns (AAFC) 1946-49; Cleveland Browns 1950-56
LENNY MOORE, Halfback, Baltimore Colts, 1956-1967

1974 **TONY CANADEO,** Halfback, Green Bay Packers 1941-44, 1946-1952
BILL GEORGE, Linebacker, Chicago Bears 1952-1965; L.A. Rams 1966
LOU GROZA, Tackle-Kicker, Cleveland Browns (AAFC) 1946-49; Cleveland Browns 1950-59, 1961-67
DICK (NIGHT TRAIN) LANE, Defensive Back, L.A. Rams 1952-53; Chicago Cardinals 1954-59; Detroit Lions 1960-65

1973 **RAYMOND BERRY,** End, Baltimore Colts 1955-1967
JIM PARKER, Guard-Tackle, Baltimore Colts 1957-1967
JOE SCHMIDT, Linebacker, Detroit Lions 1953-1965

1972 **LAMAR HUNT,** Team Owner, Dallas Texans 1960-62; Kansas City Chiefs 1963-present
GINO MARCHETTI, Defensive End, Dallas Texans 1952; Baltimore Colts 1953-1964, 1966
OLLIE MATSON, Halfback, Chicago Cardinals 1952, 1954-58; L.A. Rams 1959-1962; Detroit Lions 1963; Philadelphia Eagles 1964-66
CLARENCE (ACE) PARKER, Quarterback, Brooklyn Dodgers 1937-1941; Boston Yanks 1945; NY Yankees (AAFC) 1946

1971 **JIM BROWN,** Fullback, Cleveland Browns 1957-1965
BILL HEWITT, End, Chicago Bears 1932-36; Philadelphia Eagles 1937-39; Phil-Pitt 1943
FRANK (BRUISER) KINARD, Tackle, Brooklyn Dodgers-Tigers 1938-1944; N.Y. Yankees (AAFC) 1946-47
VINCE LOMBARDI, Coach, Green Bay Packers 1959-1967; Washington Redskins 1969
ANDY ROBUSTELLI, Defensive End, L.A. Rams 1951-55; N.Y. Giants 1956-1964
Y.A. TITTLE, Quarterback, Baltimore Colts (AAFC) 1948-49; Baltimore Colts 1950; San Francisco 49ers 1951-1960; N.Y. Giants 1961-64
NORM VAN BROCKLIN, Quarterback, L.A. Rams 1949-1957; Philadelphia Eagles 1958-1960

1970 **JACK CHRISTIANSEN,** Defensive Back, Detroit Lions 1951-58
TOM FEARS, End, L.A. Rams 1948-1956
HUGH McELHENNY, Halfback, San Francisco 49ers 1952-1960; Minnesota Vikings 1961-62; N.Y. Giants 1963; Detroit Lions 1964

PETE PIHOS, End, Philadelphia Eagles 1947-1955

1969 **GLEN (TURK) EDWARDS,** Tackle, Boston Braves 1932; Boston Redskins 1933-36; Washington Redskins 1937-1940
EARLE (GREASY) NEALE, Coach, Philadelphia Eagles 1941-42, 1944-1950; co-coach, Phil-Pitt 1943
LEO NOMELLINI, Defensive Tackle, San Francisco 49ers 1950-1963
JOE PERRY, Fullback, San Francisco 49ers (AAFC) 1948-49; San Francisco 49ers 1950-1960, 1963; Baltimore Colts 1961-62
ERNIE STAUTNER, Defensive Tackle, Pittsburgh Steelers 1950-1963

1968 **CLIFF BATTLES,** Halfback, Boston Braves 1932; Boston Redskins 1933-36; Washington Redskins 1937
ART DONOVAN, Defensive Tackle, Baltimore Colts 1950; N.Y. Yanks 1951; Dallas Texans 1952; Baltimore Colts 1953-1961
ELROY (CRAZYLEGS) HIRSCH, Halfback-End, Chicago Rockets (AAFC) 1946-48; L.A. Rams 1949-1957
WAYNE MILLNER, End, Boston Redskins 1936; Washington Redskins 1937-1941, 1945
MARION MOTLEY, Fullback, Cleveland Browns (AAFC) 1946-49; Cleveland Browns 1950-53; Pittsburgh Steelers 1955
CHARLEY TRIPPI, Halfback, Chicago Cardinals 1947-1955
ALEX WOJCIECHOWICZ, Center, Detroit Lions 1938-1946; Philadelphia Eagles 1946-1950

1967 **CHUCK BEDNARIK,** Center-Linebacker, Philadelphia Eagles 1949-1962
CHARLES W. BIDWELL, SR., Team Owner, Chicago Cardinals 1933-1943; Card-Pitt 1944; Chicago Cardinals 1945-47
PAUL BROWN, Coach, Cleveland Browns (AAFC) 1946-49; Cleveland Browns 1950-1962; Cincinnati Bengals 1968-1975
BOBBY LAYNE, Quarterback, Chicago Bears 1948; N.Y. Bulldogs 1949; Detroit Lions 1950-58; Pittsburgh Steelers 1958-1962
DAN REEVES, Team Owner, Cleveland Rams 1941-45; L.A. Rams 1946-1971
KEN STRONG, Halfback, Staten Island Stapletons 1929-1932; N.Y. Giants 1933-35; N.Y. Yanks (AFL) 1936-37; N.Y. Giants 1939, 1944-47
JOE STYDAHAR, Tackle, Chicago Bears 1936-1942, 1945-46
EMLEN TUNNELL, Safety, N.Y. Giants 1948-1958; Green Bay Packers 1959-1961

1966 **BILL DUDLEY,** Halfback, Pittsburgh Steelers 1942, 1945-46; Detroit Lions 1947-49; Washington Redskins 1950-51, 1953
JOE GUYON, Halfback, Canton Bulldogs 1920; Cleveland Indians 1921; Oorang Indians 1922-23; Rock Island, Ill., Independents 1924; Kansas City Cowboys 1924-25; N.Y. Giants 1927
ARNIE HERBER, Quarterback, Green Bay Packers 1930-1940; N.Y. Giants 1944-45
WALTER KIESLING, Guard-Coach, Duluth Eskimos 1926-27, Pottsville Maroons 1928; Chicago Cardinals 1929-1933; Chicago Bears 1934; Green Bay Packers 1935-36; Pittsburgh Pirates 1937-38; coach, Pittsburgh Steelers 1939-1942; co-coach, Phil-Pitt 1943, Card-Pitt 1944; coach, Pittsburgh Steelers 1954-56
GEORGE McAFEE, Halfback, Chicago Bears 1940-41, 1945-1950
STEVE OWEN, Tackle-Coach, Kansas City Cowboys 1924-25; N.Y. Giants 1926-1930; coach, N.Y. Giants 1931-1953
HUGH (SHORTY) RAY, Supervisor of Officials 1938-1956
CLYDE (BULLDOG) TURNER, Center, Chicago Bears 1940-1952

1965 **GUY CHAMBERLIN,** End-Coach, Decatur Staleys 1920; Chicago Staleys 1921; player-coach, Canton Bulldogs 1922-23; Cleveland Bulldogs 1924; Frankford Yellowjackets 1925-26; Chicago Cardinals 1927

JOHN (PADDY) DRISCOLL, Quarterback, Decatur Staleys 1920; Chicago Cardinals 1920-25; Chicago Bears 1926-29
DAN FORTMANN, Guard, Chicago Bears 1936-1943
OTTO GRAHAM, Quarterback, Cleveland Browns (AAFC) 1946-49; Cleveland Browns 1950-55
SID LUCKMAN, Quarterback, Chicago Bears 1939-1950
STEVE VAN BUREN, Halfback, Philadelphia Eagles 1944-1951
BOB WATERFIELD, Quarterback, Cleveland Rams 1945; L.A. Rams 1946-1952

1964 **JIMMY CONZELMAN,** Quarterback-Coach-Team Owner, Decatur Staleys 1920; Rock Island, Ill., Independents 1921-22; Milwaukee Badgers 1923-24; owner-coach, Detroit Panthers 1925-26; player-coach, Providence Steamroller 1927-29; coach, Providence Steamroller 1930; Chicago Cardinals 1940-42, 1946-1948
ED HEALEY, Tackle, Rock Island, Ill., Independents 1920-22; Chicago Bears 1922-27
CLARKE HINKLE, Fullback, Green Bay Packers, 1932-1941
ROY (LINK) LYMAN, Tackle, Canton Bulldogs 1922-23, 1925; Cleveland Bulldogs 1924; Frankford Yellowjackets 1925; Chicago Bears 1926-28, 1930-31, 1933-34
MIKE MICHALSKE, Guard, N.Y. Yankees (AFL) 1926; N.Y. Yankees 1927-28; Green Bay Packers 1929-1935, 1937
ART ROONEY, Team Owner, Pittsburgh Pirates 1933-1940; Pittsburgh Steelers 1941-42, 1945-present; Phil-Pitt 1943; Card-Pitt 1944
GEORGE TRAFTON, Center, Decatur Staleys 1920; Chicago Staleys 1921; Chicago Bears 1922-1932

1963 **SAMMY BAUGH,** Quarterback, Washington Redskins 1937-1952
BERT BELL, Commissioner-Team Owner, Philadelphia Eagles 1933-1940; Pittsburgh Steelers 1941-42; Phil-Pitt 1943; Pittsburgh Steelers 1944-46; NFL Commissioner 1946-1959
JOE CARR, NFL President 1921-1939
EARL (DUTCH) CLARK, Quarterback, Portsmouth Spartans 1931-32; Detroit Lions 1934-38
RED GRANGE, Halfback, Chicago Bears 1925; N.Y. Yankees (AFL) 1926; N.Y. Yankees 1927; Chicago Bears 1929-1934
GEORGE HALAS, End-Coach-Team Owner, Decatur Staleys 1920; Chicago Staleys 1921; Chicago Bears 1922-29; coach, Chicago Bears 1933-1942; 1946-1955, 1958-1967; owner, Chicago Bears 1920-1984
MEL HEIN, Center, N.Y. Giants 1931-1945
WILBUR (PETE) HENRY, Tackle, Canton Bulldogs 1920-23; N.Y. Giants 1927; Pottsville Maroons 1927-28
CAL HUBBARD, Tackle, N.Y. Giants 1927-28; Green Bay Packers 1929-1933, 1935; N.Y. Giants 1936; Pittsburgh Pirates 1936
DON HUTSON, End, Green Bay Packers 1935-1945
EARL (CURLY) LAMBEAU, Coach, Green Bay Packers 1919-1949; Chicago Cardinals 1950-51; Washington Redskins 1952-53
TIM MARA, Team Owner, N.Y. Giants 1925-1959
GEORGE PRESTON MARSHALL, Team Owner, Boston Braves 1932; Boston Redskins 1933-36; Washington Redskins 1937-1969
JOHNNY BLOOD (McNALLY), Halfback, Milwaukee Badgers 1925-26; Duluth Eskimos 1926-27; Pottsville Maroons 1928; Green Bay Packers 1929-1933; Pittsburgh Pirates 1934; Green Bay Packers 1935-36; player-coach, Pittsburgh Pirates 1937-39
BRONKO NAGURSKI, Fullback, Chicago Bears 1930-37, 1943
ERNIE NEVERS, Fullback, Duluth Eskimos 1926-1927; Chicago Cardinals 1929-1931
JIM THORPE, Halfback, Canton Bulldogs 1920; Cleveland Indians 1921; Oorang Indians 1922-23; Toledo Maroons 1923; Rock Island, Ill., Independents 1924; N.Y. Giants 1925; Canton Bulldogs 1926; Chicago Cardinals 1928

NUMBER-ONE DRAFT CHOICES

Season	Team	Player	Position	College
1985	Buffalo	Bruce Smith	DE	Virginia Tech
1984	New England	Irving Fryar	WR	Nebraska
1983	Baltimore	John Elway	QB	Stanford
1982	New England	Kenneth Sims	DT	Texas
1981	New Orleans	George Rogers	RB	South Carolina
1980	Detroit	Billy Sims	RB	Oklahoma
1979	Buffalo	Tom Cousineau	LB	Ohio State
1978	Houston	Earl Campbell	RB	Texas
1977	Tampa Bay	Ricky Bell	RB	Southern California
1976	Tampa Bay	Lee Roy Selmon	DE	Oklahoma
1975	Atlanta	Steve Bartkowski	QB	California
1974	Dallas	Ed Jones	DE	Tennessee State
1973	Houston	John Matuszak	DE	Tampa
1972	Buffalo	Walt Patulski	DE	Notre Dame
1971	New England	Jim Plunkett	QB	Stanford
1970	Pittsburgh	Terry Bradshaw	QB	Louisiana Tech
1969	Buffalo (AFL)	O.J. Simpson	RB	Southern California
1968	Minnesota	Ron Yary	T	Southern California
1967	Baltimore	Bubba Smith	DT	Michigan State
1966	Atlanta	Tommy Nobis	LB	Texas
	Miami (AFL)	Jim Grabowski	RB	Illinois
1965	New York Giants	Tucker Frederickson	HB	Auburn
	Houston (AFL)	Lawrence Elkins	E	Baylor
1964	San Francisco	Dave Parks	E	Texas Tech
	Boston (AFL)	Jack Concannon	QB	Boston College
1963	Los Angeles	Terry Baker	QB	Oregon State
	Kansas City (AFL)	Buck Buchanan	DT	Grambling
1962	Washington	Ernie Davis	HB	Syracuse
	Oakland (AFL)	Roman Gabriel	QB	North Carolina State
1961	Minnesota	Tommy Mason	HB	Tulane
	Buffalo (AFL)	Ken Rice	G	Auburn
1960	Los Angeles	Billy Cannon	RB	Louisiana State
	(AFL had no formal first pick)			
1959	Green Bay	Randy Duncan	QB	Iowa
1958	Chicago Cardinals	King Hill	QB	Rice
1957	Green Bay	Paul Hornung	HB	Notre Dame
1956	Pittsburgh	Gary Glick	DB	Colorado A&M
1955	Baltimore	George Shaw	QB	Oregon
1954	Cleveland	Bobby Garrett	QB	Stanford
1953	San Francisco	Harry Babcock	E	Georgia
1952	Los Angeles	Bill Wade	QB	Vanderbilt
1951	New York Giants	Kyle Rote	HB	Southern Methodist
1950	Detroit	Leon Hart	E	Notre Dame
1949	Philadelphia	Chuck Bednarik	C	Pennsylvania
1948	Washington	Harry Gilmer	QB	Alabama
1947	Chicago Bears	Bob Fenimore	HB	Oklahoma A&M
1946	Boston	Frank Dancewicz	QB	Notre Dame
1945	Chicago Cardinals	Charley Trippi	HB	Georgia
1944	Boston	Angelo Bertelli	QB	Notre Dame
1943	Detroit	Frank Sinkwich	HB	Georgia
1942	Pittsburgh	Bill Dudley	HB	Virginia
1941	Chicago Bears	Tom Harmon	HB	Michigan
1940	Chicago Cardinals	George Cafego	HB	Tennessee
1939	Chicago Cardinals	Ki Aldrich	C	Texas Christian
1938	Cleveland	Corbett Davis	FB	Indiana
1937	Philadelphia	Sam Francis	FB	Nebraska
1936	Philadelphia	Jay Berwanger	HB	Chicago